INDOCHINA
—Now and Then—

INDOCHINA
—Now and Then—

George Fetherling

DUNDURN
TORONTO

Project Editor: Michael Carroll
Copy Editor: Shannon Whibbs
Design: Jesse Hooper
Printer: Marquis

Library and Archives Canada Cataloguing in Publication

Fetherling, George
    Indochina now and then / by George Fetherling.

ISBN 978-1-55488-425-4
Also issued in electronic formats.

    1. Fetherling, George,- --Travel--Indochina. 2. Indochina--Description and travel. 3. Indochina--Colonial influence. 4. French--Indochina. I. Title.

DS535.F47 2009   915.904   C2009-903000-4

1 2 3 4 5   16 15 14 13 12

We acknowledge the support of the **Canada Council for the Arts** and the **Ontario Arts Council** for our publishing program. We also acknowledge the financial support of the **Government of Canada** through the **Canada Book Fund** and **Livres Canada Books**, and the **Government of Ontario** through the **Ontario Book Publishing Tax Credit** and the **Ontario Media Development Corporation**.

Care has been taken to trace the ownership of copyright material used in this book. The author and the publisher welcome any information enabling them to rectify any references or credits in subsequent editions.

J. Kirk Howard, President

Portions of this book have appeared in earlier versions in *Diplomat* and *Geist*.

Printed and bound in Canada.
www.dundurn.com

Dundurn	Gazelle Book Services Limited	Dundurn
3 Church Street, Suite 500	White Cross Mills	2250 Military Road
Toronto, Ontario, Canada	High Town, Lancaster, England	Tonawanda, NY
M5E 1M2	LA1 4XS	U.S.A. 14150

À la mémoire de Dale Singer Fetherling, 1941–2011

— ONE OF THE THIRTY-SIX STREETS —

Every now and then, whenever I have accumulated sufficient airline points, I go to Southeast Asia, for though it is changing so rapidly as to make one dizzy, it is also a place where the past is never hard to find. On two of these trips, I had it in mind to see what remained of French influence and culture in France's three former colonies in the region: Cambodia, Laos, and Vietnam. The objective seemed most obtainable on one of the journeys when I was travelling with my friend M, who speaks French with complete ease and fluency and no discernible English accent. We had a wonderful long stay there, traipsing about by foot, car, subway, rail, cyclo, longtail boat, and, in one brief instance, elephant. But despite all our persistent and sometimes ingenious field research, we found little evidence of what Vietnamese call "the French Time" or at least none that was extraordinary or even surprising. The nadir of our hopeful expectation came when M discovered that the corporate head office of Peugeot Auto (Asie) Ltée, or whatever it's called, seemed to shelter no one who has even as little of the French language as I do.

On another trip I will also recall in these pages, one undertaken a few years later when I happened to be travelling alone, I had a strange little low-level epiphany. I was in a building in Hanoi, in the area of Old Quarter called the Thirty-Six Streets (because in earlier times each one was home to a particular type of shop). Some of the buildings are quite old indeed, though dating them precisely is difficult, as until fairly recently architectural styles changed very slowly. What the structure I was in may once have been, I didn't know. At the moment, it was a bar. As time wore on, I found myself alone in the gents' loo with another foreigner: an American, I thought at once, and one who was looking a bit grizzled and unshaven. I was about to wash my hands at one of two adjoining basins; he was bending over the other one to splash water on his face. The spigots were ancient. He turned on the one marked *C* and muttered a foul Midwestern oath. He had expected cold water to come out.

The lesson was that only a few traces of the French imperial mission survived the destruction of a French army in 1954 at the remote town of Dien Bien Phu in the far northwest of Vietnam, near the Lao border: a defeat that opened the way for the U.S. misadventure in Vietnam the following decade. But now the latter war too is much less a fact of living memory than it is a subject for patriotic schoolroom recitation. This change speaks to the high birth rate in Asia and the low one in the West. But of course it also speaks to the very nature of time itself.

— LANDS OF CHARM AND CRUELTY —

In a period that still seems to me not all that long ago, it was possible to find early postcards from Southeast Asia in the booksellers' stalls along the Seine in Paris. They usually cost only a few francs (there were no euros in those days). The photos on them were interesting, because, without quite meaning to do so, they revealed a great deal about the indigenous cultures in that part of the world and their struggles with European colonialism. In Amsterdam, I suppose, a person as determined as I used to be could have found picture postcards that Dutch businessmen and administrators had sent back home from what's now Indonesia. Portobello Road and many other places in London must have hidden British ones that their authors had posted from various places in the empire. Having come of age during the Vietnam War — which, to avoid confusion, I will hereafter refer to as the American War, the way the Vietnamese do — I was interested in those that came from Indochina.

Even the term Indochina is not without confusion. Until recent decades, Indochina was also known as Farther India. Both names referred to the peninsular part of southeastern Asia, the territory east of India and south of China: Burma, Thailand (formerly Siam), Laos, Cambodia, Vietnam, and Malaysia (formerly Malaya). These were places that for great stretches of history had not only fought one another almost constantly, but were subject to the cultures of both India and China. Religion naturally occasioned much strife in this region, one which Stan Sesson, an American journalist a hundred years later, perfectly named "the lands of charm and cruelty." Eventually of course, Hinduism waned in these areas while Buddhism ascended and Islam became the religion of Malaysia and a strong presence in certain other regions.

The era of European colonialism brought the British. They wanted to expand their control of India eastward, across Indochina, until they reached China proper, and then find ways of moving northward into that vast market. The French had a similar goal, but a different strategy. They wished to get a toehold in Cochinchina, the southernmost portion of the three kingdoms of what's now Vietnam, where the Mekong finally empties into the South China Sea after a journey of five thousand kilometres from the Tibetan Plateau. They reasoned that if they controlled its mouth, they could follow the river straight up through Cambodia and Laos into southern China. When France captured Saigon in 1862, it believed it had the makings of great new entrepôt, a new Shanghai, as many said, that would allow them to dominate the Mekong and make it a commercial artery rivalling the Yangzi in importance. In 1863, they signed a treaty that gave Cambodia the status of a French protectorate. Three years later, a major scientific and commercial expedition was dispatched under Ernest Doudart de Lagrée and Francis Garnier. Their report, published in 1873 as *Voyage d'exploration en Indo-Chine*, created a sensation in Paris, as it contained the first detailed study of the great "lost" city of Angkor. But their harrowing journey through territory virtually unknown to the West also resulted in the discovery of the Khong Falls on the Cambodia-Laos border, which made steam navigation all the way to China impossible. French plans then shifted to constructing a railway once they had acquired the middle and northern kingdoms of Vietnam: Annam, whose capital was Hué, and Tonkin, whose capital was Hanoi. The plan was never entirely successful, whereas today, the People's Republic of China is building a high-speed rail system that will run from Kunming, in Yunnan Province, all the way down to Singapore.

France was demoralized at the time by its defeat in the Franco-Prussian War of 1870 and hoped to find solace, and much-needed revenues, in a new wave of colonial acquisition. The problem was the Thais, who controlled much of Laos. This obstacle wasn't resolved until 1893 when another treaty gave France the land on the east side of the Mekong, while the Thais retained that on the west. Just as in the British Empire, there are colonies and then there are *colonies*: a heavily stratified system based on the amount of local political autonomy. A territory, a protectorate, a colony, and other fine distinctions — they all meant different things. French Indochina (*Indochine française* — the term did not become official until 1897) was never technically a part of France itself, as Algeria was. It was a ragged collection of little states, gathered by dubious means. France pledged to hold them together for commercial and political purposes, but was also forced to keep them separate and on unequal footing so as to prevent them from joining forces in an uprising.

The reason why Vietnam is such an easy place for Westerners to explore is that the French approved and accelerated the process by which the Roman alphabet supplanted Chinese characters there, a transition that also underscored the separateness of Vietnam from neighbouring Cambodia and Laos. The tactic recalls how, in the days of the African slave trade, whites would often bring together slaves of different linguistic groups, hoping in that way to minimize talk of revolt. Cambodia and Laos have their own scripts derived from Sanskrit and Pali. Both are especially difficult for Westerners to master, however beautiful they may be to look at. (The Khmer script of Cambodia enjoyed somewhat of a vogue in the West when Angelina Jolie had a sample of it tattooed on her lower back.)

The French nationals who went to French Indochina to work, to administer or to save souls were just as diverse and just as predictable as the British who served the nineteenth century's other great European empire. There is much to be learned about their roles from such excellent and easily translated books as Charles Meyer's *Les Français en Indochine 1860–1910* (1985). And it's also fascinating to see how often and variously French Indochina popped up in both the serious and popular cultures of France. With what earnestness the readers and cinephiles in the 1950s and 1960s regarded Indochina's most famous expat artist, Marguerite Duras, a Saigon native. With what amusement Parisians in the 1920s and 1930s listened to Josephine Baker, wearing one of her potassium-rich costumes, sing "La Petite Tonkinoise."

So it was that following Dien Bien Phu that the reality of "French Indochina" ceased to exist and even the simple words *Indochina* and *Indochine* fell into disrepute. When the United States became interested in the area following the French defeat, it carefully adopted the term "Southeast Asia," a usage that had two advantages: it had a broader geographical meaning, taking in many island nations, and it disguised the assumption that the United States was taking over where the French had left off.

☙ ✳ ❧

— SOUVENIRS —

Sometimes it almost seems as though every French national going out to the colonies (*territoires d'outre-mer*) and the like, whether for the civil service, the military, or the Catholic Church, or for some business concern such as the Michelin rubber plantations, felt the same urge to send photographic evidence to contacts in Europe, overwhelming them with proof of the region's beauty and presumed strangeness and barbarity. Evidently such postcards were also exchanged between and among the various French colonies round the world. As an accumulator (*collector* is too dignified a word) of these early views of Indochina, I made my biggest discovery in a junk store (*curio shop* sounds way too grand) in Tahiti.

Picture postcards came about, slowly, with the daguerreotype in the middle of the nineteenth century. The British photographer and printer Francis Frith (1822–98) is one person strongly associated with the idea. He specialized in views of Middle Eastern landmarks. Yet in Europe and America, just as by extension in Southeast Asia, such privately produced photographic postcards, as distinct from those issued by government post offices with or without images, became the rage only around 1900, the year that Eastman Kodak introduced the first Brownie cameras. With that invention, anyone could be a photographer, needing only a local printer to become a postcard artist. Of my own accumulation, from which I have chosen sixty to illustrate this little text, the majority seem to come from the first decade of the twentieth century, judging by the postmarks found on some of them. It is important to remember that these were snapshots that Europeans took for their own purposes and that they reflect what Europeans believed they knew about Indochina and wished others to believe. Local populations had different priorities when they caused themselves (rather than permitted themselves) to be photographed. This is one reason such postcards have long been studied by scholars in the field of postcolonial theory.

There was of course a demand for studio portraiture in sophisticated cities such as Hanoi, Hué, and Saigon. In small communities in remote regions, the pretensions of the ruling elites were similar, but the facilities to satisfy them were not always first-rate. According to the city's official historian, Battambang, western Cambodia, in 1907, had only "one photographer, but lacking electricity, photographs were taken outdoors." The photographer was Chinese. People engaged him:

> to come to their homes to take pictures but the photography apparatus of that time was large and it was difficult to carry up and down. Only the important and wealthy were able to have photographs taken due to the expense. Commoners dared not have their photograph taken because they believed that the camera was able to take human blood and shorten their lives, and they were certain that most of those who had their photograph taken would die a few months later.

The French were not being altogether disingenuous when they maintained that their empire was more than just a giant commercial venture but was also a *mission civilisatrice*. But the so-called civilizing ran in both directions. The French imposed their own ways of doing things in areas as different as religion, public education, and civil service examinations — in fact, the whole gamut of manners and practices that go together to make up a society. But French linguists, anthropologists, archaeologists, curators — scholars of all types — studied and catalogued the cultures they found in the various colonies.

They made them widely known and in doing so helped to preserve them even more than they imperilled them. The people who took the photographs in this book must have had baser motives. The images tell us a great deal about how the people in French Indochina dressed, worked, and deported themselves. But they also pander to the timeless appeal of sex and crime.

Postcard makers overlooked few opportunities to manufacture eroticism from the merely exotic. One image likely to be found in any large collection of Cambodian and Lao pictures will show bare-breasted dancers of the classical ballet that is important to those cultures. These were attempts to blur the distinction between French colonial postcards and "French postcards" and thus claim a place in art. The same applied to European postcards of bare-breasted women simply going about their daily labours in African countries, the Netherlands East Indies, Burma, Malaya, the Straits Settlements (Malacca, Penang, Singapore, and Labuan), Sarawak, Sabah, Brunei, the Philippines, the Pacific Islands in general, and so on. One also sometimes sees bare-breasted Chinese and Japanese women in postcards of the period, but they tend to be posed carefully with a European eye, without much illusion of candidness. As for crime photos, Indochina and other European colonies provided much opportunity to exploit another type of voyeurism by recording whippings, beheadings, and even crucifixions (a specialty in the area near the northern borders of British Burma).

The demand for postcards of Indochina may have reached a peak after the Great War, though certainly it was still in force during the 1920s, when tokens of the Indochinese colonies were quite popular in Paris. The appeal lingered on until the 1930s, when supplanted by more traditional tastes — colourful landmarks or scenes of obvious natural beauty; in other words, postcards like those from everywhere else. That the more exotic and grisly style of postcards began to disappear during the time of greatest civil unrest against the French regime cannot be mere coincidence. In 1917, Ho Chi Minh, having taken up exile in France, began agitating against the French presence in Vietnam. In 1920, he joined the French Communist Party, and then went to study in the Soviet Union before being assigned to the East. In Hong Kong in 1930, he established the Vietnamese Communist Party, followed by more years of study and agitation in various cultures. It wasn't until 1940, after being away for three decades, that he returned to Vietnam, for he could sense that, with the Second World War underway, the Vichy regime in France would sell out his country to the Japanese. He was right, of course. Where the World War left off, the war against the French colonial system started up. As Charles de Gaulle later said, "It was a dirty business on both sides." The rest is history — and geography.

— UP THE PENINSULA —

I have long remained loyal to the cliché that the story of getting to the destination is at least as interesting as that of the destination itself. The last time I was in Singapore, I arrived aboard a cargo ship. We had anchored in the roads, and the next morning proceeded into the harbour with no sense of shame. There were fifty or so other vessels there, all of them, viewed from a distance, were magnificent compared to our own. This time I arrived during the global recession when it was estimated that 10 percent of the world's deep-water cargo vessels were lying there for want of business, and I saw them only briefly and from above, for now I was travelling on Singapore Airlines, the best use to which anyone's frequent-flyer points can possibly be put. Singapore is about twenty hours from Vancouver. It was midnight (but of which day?)

when I looked out the window of the Airbus 340-500 and saw vivid clusters of lights scattered everywhere. The effect was something like firefly-patterned wallpaper in a room that is otherwise utterly dark. Then I saw the unmistakable Singapore Flyer, the enormous illuminated Ferris wheel-type contraption that emulates the Millennium Wheel in London. We would be landing soon. The intercom came alive with a slight crackle. One of the uniformly charming Singaporean flight attendants (they memorize the passengers' names in advance) reminded us in a sweet Audrey Hepburn voice that bringing illegal drugs into the country is punishable by death and thank-you-for-flying-with-us-this-evening. Like my former ship, a rusty old hulk indeed, I knew that however much I try, I will never be well enough dressed to be in Singapore.

What everyone everywhere seems to know about Singapore is true, but it is never enough to break through one of the walls on the other side of which lies a more relevant understanding. Yes, it's a tiny round island, 43.5 by 22.5 kilometres, once one of the jewels of the British Empire. That status was not in dispute until 1942. Singapore's main defences faced south, toward the sea, not north, across the little Johor Straight that separates it from what was then the rest of Malaya. The Japanese came down from the north. They overran the British and Canadian garrison and slaughtered many of the residents, military and civilian alike.

Politics were often rocky in the few decades following the war, particularly as Malaya was in the bitter bloody process of becoming the independent Malaysia of today. The transitional structure between plain Malaya and the new Malaysia was called the Malay Federation, of which Singapore was a part. But the two entities broke off relations, leaving Singapore to go it alone as a city-state, which, in an informal sense, it had been for a long time. Since then, Singapore has been run by a series of authoritarian rulers, most famously by a father and his son, with a place-holder in between. It is prosperous, modern, beautiful, safe, business-oriented, and, yes, a bit rigid in matters of social behaviour, though far less so now than just a few years ago. It is no longer a crime to carry chewing gum into the country, but the government still makes a fuss when criticized in the Western press, from time to time restricting or banning the *Economist* or the *Asian Wall Street Journal.* Conversely, casinos have been legal since 2005: quite a change. Over the years, I have met a number of Canadians who have taken up teaching positions there for a year or so. I've always envied them. What else can I report? I was surprised to see local books about Singapore prostitutes being freely published and sold. It seemed obvious (but not blatant) that gay love and lesbian love, while forbidden in theory always, are practised without commotion at least on the weekends.

I wasn't simply wandering round Singapore blindly and without aim, accumulating such offhand observations. I had no intention of loitering in the Raffles Hotel, worshipping its bar as the birthplace of the Singapore Sling, the way Western visitors enjoy doing. I had a contact to make. She is a friend of one of the Canadian teachers alluded to above, and her name is Evelyn Yang. She and I had never met, but I knew that she possessed Local Knowledge, that most valuable commodity required by travellers, for she is a native-born Singaporean whose family had come to the city from the fast-disappearing rural areas on the north side of the island where they farmed. She and I hit it off at once. She took me walking to illustrate how Singapore's demography has evolved in such interesting ways.

Despite its slowly unbending reputation for clean-cut repression, Singapore is a society of expert compromisers. It has to be. Seventy-five percent of the people are ethnic Chinese, jumbling Buddhist, Confucian, and Daoist beliefs, while 15 percent are Malays who practise Islam. The final 10 percent are South Asian, mostly Tamils. The demographic arithmetic under which Singapore operates so well is based on some ethnic and religious equations fundamentally different from those found anywhere else in this part of the world.

Evelyn pointed out old Sanskrit inscriptions on buildings that were most definitely Chinese. These were small emblems of the fact that if the French of Indochina had to find a way to unify Tonkin, Annam, Cochinchina, Laos, and Cambodia without letting themselves be ganged up on, then the British in Singapore, all the way back to the arrival of Sir Thomas Stamford Raffles in 1819, had to learn how to profit from overwhelming numbers of Chinese of wildly different origins. As policies developed over time, this task came down to shuffling the deck to make separate districts for the Chinese as well as for the Malays and Indians. But the plan didn't end there. It was also necessary to keep Chinese from squabbling amongst themselves. As Raffles had proposed as early as 1822, whole neighbourhoods were set aside for people from particular provinces. In such groupings, predictably, the matter of one's exact ancestral origins on the map were inseparable from the question of which dialect one spoke. Speakers of Hokkienese were centred on certain streets, speakers of Hainanese on others. These in turn were quite separate from, say, those whose tongue was Cantonese (which in old Singapore was often called Macao Chinese, indicating those individuals' connection to the former Portuguese colony below Hong Kong).

"These groupings lasted far into modern days," Evelyn said. "But they fell away, a little bit at a time — like farm land being sold off to property developers." The metaphor made her sound wistful.

But it was a different set of policies that pushed Singapore into the contemporary world. For years, the British had been promising that the Chinese would hold real political power in the run-up to Independence in 1959 and of course thereafter. In Singapore and the rest of colonial Malaya, Chinese residents were given ever bigger roles as a way of making them feel like important stakeholders. Let subjects become fully engaged citizens (and let small-business owners become capitalists). According to the logic of Whitehall, that would keep them from giving aid to the communists, particularly those active next door, on the Malay Peninsula itself. As it happened, this plan worked surprisingly well, the usual turmoil and bloodshed notwithstanding. The Singaporean Chinese evidently felt a diminished sense of Chinese nationalism based on race and a greater sense of being Singaporeans in particular. As certain sociologists would say, there has been a lessening of the sojourner attitude. This was in contrast to what, in recent years especially, seems to have been the emotional trend in many other segments of the worldwide Chinese diaspora. The Chinese in Singapore get along rather well as Singaporeans. As Evelyn said to me over lunch one day, "I speak Hokkienese. My husband is Fuzhou-speaking. At home, we use English." She laughed at the wonderful incongruity of it all.

Yet our midday meal, paradoxically, was quite nationalistic in feel, owing to the extremity of the multicultural impulse behind it. We were at a tiny spotless restaurant with a feng shui mirror over the front door to misdirect bad spirits. It served Peranakan food, which is sometimes called Nyonya. This cuisine is not fusion, a term that suggests that elements have been combined artificially or at least deliberately. Rather, it is a style of cookery that has risen in organic fashion from various traditions over the five centuries or so that Europeans have been doing business in coastal Asia. Just as British, Dutch, and Portuguese traders mated with Chinese, Malays et al., so did Malay curries take up with Indian spices and Siamese herbs until there no longer seemed anything strange in the result. Described in theory this way, Peranakan doesn't sound all that unusual. But several key ingredients local to the region make it nearly irreproducible anywhere else. One is *buah keluak* (in English: candlenut), which grows mostly in Indonesia and Malaysia and is poisonous until reasoned with. In one dish, its kernel is pulverized, sweetened, salted, and mixed with *very* spicy chicken or pork (the latter indicating that Muslims avoid Peranakan meals).

Like other sophisticated women in Singapore, at least in my observation and experience, Evelyn was apparently not affected in the least by the reckless use of scandalously strong spices nor by the fact that walking through the streets was like exercising in a steam room. She was crisp, pressed, stylish, and poised. I imagined she always was. I never quite got up the courage to ask her what her Chinese name was. Living in Canada, where a quarter of the population is from somewhere else — and residing as I do in one of the two cities where the figure is 50 percent — I know that scratching the veneer of another person's reinvention is the essence of poor etiquette. Evelyn was Evelyn, with her perfect hair, Gucci bag, and (here I am only guessing) $700 shoes. In one of our talks, however, there did come a point where, bolstered by context, I thought it safe to inquire about how her family made out during the Japanese occupation, so many years before her birth. At first she sidestepped the question with diplomatic ease. Later, on her own accord, she returned to it, and recounted horrible scenes of rape and death as she had learned about them from her grandmother. "She could not forgive, she could not forget."

In another two days, I would be crossing over into Malaysia. Bypassing Kuala Lumpur if possible (for I have bad memories of the place — details to follow), I would make my way up Thailand to rendezvous with my friend Christopher G. Moore, the thriller writer. Many of his books are set in Bangkok, though his experience of Southeast Asia overall is long, wide, and deep. He has expert Local Knowledge written all over him.

Before I left Singapore, however, Evelyn wanted to take me to Thian Hock Keng. I believed I knew why. This temple in the middle of Chinatown is the perfect illustration of how Singapore's past and present connect in the way they do. For years, Thian Hock Keng, built in 1840 and thus one of the oldest buildings in Singapore, was the largest structure on the island. It took generations to complete, and the long-term commitment of poor immigrants as well as wealthy *min* businessmen. It is located on Telok Ayer Street, in the centre of the area that was so long ago decreed the Hokkien heart-land. No doubt the neighbourhood always has been densely populated, but originally it must have been quite compact in area. I presume that the fact that a thoroughfare named Synagogue Street is only two or three blocks to the north suggests how closely it once bordered another very different community. I wish I knew about more the historical relation-ship between Jews and Singapore. What I do know is that the funeral customs of some Singaporean Chinese are quite close to those of Judaism. Mourners perform a ritual very much like sitting shiva. Mirrors are either draped in cloth or turned to the wall.

Thian Hock Keng follows the architectural conventions of Chinese palaces, with its upswept roofs, courtyards, and red-lacquered rooms with exposed beams. To say the least, it has multiple layers and levels of religious and mythological adornment, including stone windows decorated with a bat motif. Bats, whether living or symbolic, are valued because in Mandarin the word for bat (*fu*) is pronounced the same as *fu*, meaning good fortune. The complex faces south, and I would guess was once closer to the waterfront than it is now. In any case, its main hall is a shrine to Ma Zu, the sea goddess, whose day is the twenty-third day of the third lunar month. Workers either coming down from China to earn a living or returning home after a lifetime of labour would go there to give thanks for a safe sea journey or to pray for one. Over time, an assortment of other important deities, Confucian and Daoist, as well as Buddhist, protected the temple, and the place lost — outgrew, but not abandoned — its association with migrants. It became an important religious centre for Singapore Chinese, regardless of geographic ties of linguistic allegiance. It became, in fact, the very symbol of a strong, permanent, and self-sustaining Singapore that grew out of the sojourner experience.

On entering, I left my shoes on the stone steps, as one does. On leaving, I thought for a moment that they had been stolen. But no, an attendant of some sort, a surly fellow, had separated them from the shoes of Asian worshippers on the topmost step and placed them on one much lower down, indicating what in his view was my less than elevated status. I picked them up and carried them a short distance away before putting them on, so I wouldn't give further offence by tying the laces on temple property. He glowered at me as I did so. Evelyn betrayed no reaction whatsoever. Such was her natural dignity that she refused to take notice.

— DODGE CITY R&R —

Years ago, I was in Kuala Lumpur for a conference when I was struck so horribly ill with some consciousness-attacking disease (it felt as though it must be a disease) that I rang down to the manager of the hotel. I was phoning from a supine position, as I was too weak to sit up. The manager was Malaysian, of course. I begged him to find an English-speaking doctor who might be persuaded to come examine me. During his long pause, I thought I could hear him thinking: *Hmmm, I suppose I must do so, for if this big nose dies in 401, I shall have to lower the rate.*

Eventually a South Asian doctor arrived wearing a lab coat and stethoscope and carrying his gladstone bag. He was followed by his nurse, also in a lab coat, pushing a large trolley with many crowded shelves of vials and bottles of assorted pills, powders, and liquids. *Ah,* I remember thinking to myself — proud that I could still think at all — *this must be one of those places where physicians enjoy a monopoly on pharmacy.* Rather than vice versa, as in some other countries in what was then still called the Third World (a term coined by a French anthropologist, Alfred Sauvy, in 1952).

In my state, I was having difficulty understanding what the doctor was saying, but mention was made of brain fever. Researching the matter some days later, after an injection of stuff into one buttock and a quite difficult flight back to Canada, I learned that this ailment primarily afflicts people in nineteenth-century English novels. I concluded that I must have had a brush with something well short of the mildest form of encephalitis. That's far too powerful a word to be using, but the episode was enough to leave me with a lingering dislike of KL. So it was that I was now in Penang instead. I left my Chinese hotel in George Town, took a short detour through Little India, and tracked down a European breakfast (how much easier adult life would be if I had acquired a tolerance for congee as a child). Then I boarded the ferry across the channel to Butterworth on the mainland.

Naturally enough, few English names have survived in Malaysia, and those that have continue only as alternatives that are used rarely. Butterworth, for example, is the seat of the province of Wellesley, which nobody calls anything other than Seberang Perai. George Town is one exception. To complicate matters, Butterworth (for William John Butterworth, governor of the Straits Settlements, 1843–55), is also known as, simply, *Bagan,* a Malay word for "pier" or "breakwater." It is an undemonstrative place of about a hundred thousand people. I made my way to the railway station where there is a taxi rank, for I was going to take a cab to Thailand. The plan was not nearly so ridiculous as it sounds, as the border is only about three hours to the north via the first-class motorway and the fare is quite inexpensive, varying a bit according to size of the car more than to length of the journey. I paid only 30 ringgit, which was about ten dollars at the time.

English is a mandatory subject in Malaysian schools. How successful the policy is I couldn't judge, but one will sometimes hear English being used as a lingua franca when members of different ethnic minorities attempt to converse with one another. I knew the driver had English for he demonstrated as much when he asked if I wished my bag put in the boot. Once we got underway, however, his mouth slammed shut and remained closed despite my repeated attempts to lure him into conversation. He was a young fellow, expressionless except in the eyes. I mentally ran through a list of Malaysian sensitivities, wondering if I had stepped on one or more of them inadvertently. On my previous visit (before I took sick) I heard a Kuala Lumpur yuppie upbraid her paying audience of foreign professionals, saying "You people come over here and expect to see jungle and rubber plantations!" She snorted contemptuously. I remembered this incident because the countryside we were driving through now didn't seem to be advancing headlong toward development. So perhaps I was simply being cast in the familiar unwanted role of despised Westerner, or maybe I was seen merely as an infidel.

Malaysia is one of those countries that doesn't like to see an Israeli stamp in your passport, but levels of Islamic strictness vary widely according to locale. Based on nothing more than how women are dressed, there are luxury shopping streets in KL that you would almost swear were in the West — precisely as one would expect in a city of 10 million. And religious tolerance is naturally highest in areas where there are so many non-Muslims to be tolerated — mostly Buddhists,

Hindus, and Daoists, of course, but also the usual mixture of bizarre little Christian sects that American missionaries usually command. Way down in Sarawak and Sabah, on the Malaysian side of what otherwise is the Indonesian state of Borneo, there are plenty of groups that practise animism and various shamanistic rituals.

The popular understanding is that fundamentalist Islam is most common along the northeastern coast of Malaysia, certainly not in the northwest where we were driving. After three hours, we pulled up to the Thai border, where I got out and crossed on foot, as required, while the driver made his own peace with the authorities and met me on the other side of the imaginary dotted line. Suddenly, as we started up again, heading toward Hat Yai, about forty minutes farther north, the driver became comparatively loquacious.

Ah, I thought to myself, *he was anxious about going through immigration and customs. He probably uses his taxi runs as a cover for low-level smuggling.* As we chatted discontinuously, however, I had an additional realization: he simply didn't like Canadians. "Canada people too *fat!*" he said. He became quite emphatic. "Too much food for Canada. Even good food bad for you in Canada." Then it was my turn to be quiet.

Many Bangkok expats on a budget come to Hat Yai every three months, usually by bus, to get their visas renewed and then re-enter their temporary country after only an hour or so in Malaysia (whereas more affluent expats fly to Singapore or Hong Kong for the same purpose). Hat Yai is at least twice the size of Butterworth and vastly more urban, but that's not to say that it is cosmopolitan. It is a border town, a little rough round the edges without being enjoyably picaresque. Mind you, I may have been catching Hat Yai at a bad moment. Certainly I was catching it at or near record high temperatures, so that my judgment may have been skewed. That being said, the city was a brownish yellow all over and seemed to be coated with a thin film of scum, like a dirty cooking pot left to soak in the sink overnight.

Although no trace of the fact appears to survive, Hat Yai was once the site of a most curious experiment in urban planning. The idea originated with Phibun Songkhram (1897–1964), who might be called the Chiang Kai-shek of Thailand. He was a military officer, trained in France, and one of the leaders of the 1932 coup that overthrew the absolute monarchy in favour of a constitutional one and foiled a subsequent counter-revolution. In 1939, the year after he became prime minister for the first time, he changed the name of Siam to Thailand — the homeland of the ethnic Thai people, but pointedly not that of the Chinese and others. Phibun was of Chinese heritage himself, but developed strongly xenophobic ideas as part and parcel of becoming a fascist dictator.

He was a Mussolini-like figure who sided with Japan during the Second World War, though some argue that letting the Japanese *use* Thailand was the only alternative to having them overrun and occupy it. One should also probably factor in the admiration with which he and many other Thais viewed Japan and its culture, as an Asian nation that had modernized itself without the slightly blessed burden of European colonialism. In principle, Asian influences were preferred to Western ones. For example, Thais tended to fear that France had designs on their country (just as the French themselves feared that the British in Burma were lusting for Laos). The Japanese *arrived* in Thailand the same day that they, by contrast, *attacked* Pearl Harbor (though the first occurred on December 7, 1941, and the other on December 8, owing to the International Date Line). Phibun thought they would be a good friend to have one day. But when the United States defeated Japan in 1945, he and his supporters became pro-American, showing their particularly American-style anti-communism by sending a small number of troops to fight in the Korean War. That was in 1950, the year that Phibun commanded that Thailand become *modern*, a word he considered a synonym for *American.*

Thailand was a different place in those days, with parts of its ancient culture quite intact. The famous Oriental Hotel in Bangkok, for example, still had no bathtubs or showers, only large brass jars of fresh water to pour over oneself. One day Phibun decreed that the country should be full of cinemas, and suddenly it was. This decision all but exterminated the ancient puppet shows, shadow-plays, and dance-dramas so central to Thai culture (though, in the last-named case, it spared the next generation of five-year-old girls from having their fingers bent back and elongated, a practice comparable to Chinese foot-binding). The frantic building of movie theatres brought American mass culture. Hollywood westerns were especially admired. Accordingly, Phibun came up with the idea of turning Hat Yai, of all places, into a replica of a Wild West town: in his view, the quintessence of modernity. Teams of researchers were hired to dig up archival photographs of such places as Dodge City.

In Hat Yai, many activities, such as kite-flying and betting on fighting-fish, were abolished, though whisky was still to be drunk the customary way, served warm in half-pint portions. Thai thoroughfares were pulled down and replaced with imitation Western main streets with board sidewalks and false-front wooden buildings, including ersatz saloons with bat-wing doors, and all that went with this new aesthetic. Hitching rails were much in evidence though Hat Yai had no horses. Local citizens were forced to wear Wild West costumes. Some were seconded to simulate bank robbers and the civilian posses that pursued them. All this was in 1952, three years prior to the opening of Walt Disney's first theme park and well before Fess Parker's appearance as Davy Crockett on American television. At the time, Hat Yai was the favourite R&R destination of Malay guerrillas from the across the border, where they were fighting their long drawn-out war for independence: a foreshadowing of the way Bangkok became such a haven for U.S. soldiers during the American War in the late 1960s and early 1970s. Perhaps because these insurgents, communists though they were, were fighting the British, they were not much interfered with in Hat Yai where, at the time, the local security forces had been issued with coonskin caps — ringed tails and all.

⊱ ✳ ⊰

— TRAIN 170, OVERNIGHT TO BANGKOK —

At 1400 hours I was waiting on the platform at Hat Yai for the overnight train to Bangkok. I was still waiting at 1430, 1500, 1530, and 1545. Between departures and arrivals, some of the women operating battered food carts left the plastic crates they used as seats and curled up on wooden benches, putting scarves over their faces as protection from the sun. Let their children tend the stands for a while. Later it would be the kids' turn to nap. All the while, weary soldiers shuffled up and down. For my part, I was feeling was quite patient, perhaps uncharacteristically so, for I already knew at least something of both the pleasures and the hardships of Southeast Asian rail travel. I was anticipating the former and resigned to the latter.

I had read about and heard about the so-called jungle train in Malaysia that departs Jerantut Station in KL and runs north-eastwardly through Kelantan, the province said to be centre for the country's most militant Islamic fundamentalists. My understanding is that it takes ten hours or so to crawl nearly five hundred kilometres through the jungle, past banana plantations and such. The destination is a small port on the South China Sea. I'm told there are always far more passengers than seats and that the atmosphere is hostile to foreigners. Hostile to everyone's health, as well; many of the windows are broken out to admit a little air. It all sounds a great deal grittier than the jungle train that used to carry crops across Costa Rica to Puerto Limon on the Caribbean, a journey I was lucky to have made before the entire right-of-way was destroyed in an earthquake. I was similarly well informed about Cambodia's now virtually non-functioning rail system a couple of decades ago, during the last phase of the country's civil war. In addition to pulling the carriages, the locomotive also pushed a flatcar ahead. When rebels in the hills would begin shooting at the train, Cambodian troops, crouching behind some sandbags on the flatcar, would send a few mortar rounds in the general direction of the enemy. Westerners enjoyed the privilege of riding the train for free, or almost for free, so long as they rode on the flatcar. Sometimes the engine would push two flatcars. The job of the first one was to trigger mines that might have been attached to the rails.

Finally, the No. 170 to Bangkok arrived and we boarded in a jumbled rush. Simply by looking out the window, one would never suspect that this train passes through such newsworthy territory. Only 8 percent of Thailand's 68 million people are Muslims, but they constitute the majority in the four provinces closest to Malaysia. These are Yala, Narathiwat, Songkhla, and Pattani, where, for six or seven years before the trip I'm describing, ethnic Malays had been fighting to make an independent Islamic state of the strictest sort. Several thousand people had been killed, some by the insurgents, some by the Thai army. Rebel tactics have included bombing nightclubs, burning schools, and knocking out power grids. Beheadings, however, are what seem to frighten Thais most of all. Each time there is a new rash of decapitations in the south, the authorities in Bangkok respond with fresh resolve and then declare victory. And so it goes.

There were no berths available when I purchased my ticket. My seat faced the rear of the train, so that I saw the landscape unravelling counter-clockwise, so to speak. The click-click of the rails was matched by the rhythm of the countryside popping up and then quickly vanishing down the right-of-way. There were big stretches of open country alternating with fields and paddies under cultivation. Safely in the distance, brown mountains. But at what seemed almost to be regular intervals little hamlets would whiz past, with a home or two, some vehicles, some buffalo, a stand selling local produce, and either a wat or a mosque. In each case, a sign announced the name of the community, but I could find no such places on the fairly detailed road atlas I had brought with me.

The carriage was full of Muslim women with diamond-shaped Malay faces, travelling in twos and threes, with baskets and tote bags full of food for the journey. I was surprised at how easily they laughed; they were having a good time, or at least making the best of a tiring trip. From across the aisle, an especially cute infant gurgled at me and I smiled in return, which obviously pleased the mother, who said something in Thai that sounded quite friendly. But this interaction brought a fierce scowl to the face of the young man sitting opposite me. He was in his late twenties and was better dressed than the other passengers, including your correspondent: well-shined shoes, tailored slacks, an expensive-looking belt, a crisp white dress shirt, a costly watch, an MP3 player jabbed in his ear. For the next few hours he stared at me: the real snake-eye treatment. Later, a food vendor passed through the carriage, doing brisk business. This was a signal for me to take my own bag of goodies from the overhead rack. I smiled and offered the other fellow some, thinking I might get at least a faint nod. He did not react. I began to wonder whether there was trouble in the offing. He was still staring when the sun woke me (and the entire complement of babies). With the exception of this one suspicious young Muslim in secular Westernized attire, everyone else was rumpled and bleary-eyed as we began rattling through the outer slums of the capital. Moments before we reached Hualamphong Station, we both stood up at the same instant, I to reach for my bag, but he to reach inside his pocket. He pulled out a tiny digital camera. Using gestures, he asked me whether he could snap my picture. I was surprised. He put his thumb and forefinger round the corner of his mouth, indicating that I should smile. I smiled. Then (finally) he smiled, and we disembarked and were individually subsumed in the morning's rush-hour crowd.

— BANGKOK NOIR —

This was the first time I'd ever gone to Bangkok by land and I felt odd not to be disoriented, as I am when arriving by plane. When you fly in across the Pacific, one of the first oddities you notice is that it's the same day as when you left, but a different date. Ah, the International Date Line: the stories I could tell you. I once arrived in Taipei to interview some government official on the wrong day, only to find that the Taiwanese didn't sigh too loudly, for they are used to such things. Another peculiarity of Bangkok is that, in my own experience at least, all flights arriving there do so at 0100 hours, regardless of their origin or the direction travelled.

I used to stay in big hotels when I could afford them, but some years ago my friend Christopher G. Moore, the expat Canadian novelist, recommended that M and I stay at a clean, cheap Indian-run hotel in Soi 8 near Nana Station, and it has been our local headquarters ever since. In its little restaurant, deserted except for me, I refreshed my taste for the *Bangkok Post* and my impatience with the other English-language daily, the *Nation*. Reading these online is simply not the same. The *Post* was founded in 1946 by an American, Alexander

MacDonald, using presses acquired at an auction of Japanese property seized after the war. MacDonald first arrived in the country by air — by parachute, actually. He was working for the CIA's predecessor, the Office of Strategic Services, helping to organize the Free Thai resistance movement in the north. I still regret that once, years ago, at an auction in aid of a Bangkok charity, I passed up one of the small maps of Thailand printed on silk that American and British operatives and pilots kept tucked inside their flight suits. I believe that the *Post*, when I became aware of its existence, was owned by the first Lord Thomson. Some people said he found it a convenient place to store his son-in-law.

In Bangkok, as in major centres all over Asia, there is life everywhere, on every street, in every shop and at all hours. For many people such as myself it is not only a key destination in its own right, but the staging area and provisioning place for incursions into Vietnam, Cambodia, Laos, Burma, and so on. It's a sprawling, polluted, congested, and deafening city of 10 million people — and twenty universities, thirty hospitals, and a recent architecture of astonishing ugliness, as the element of gigantism found in Asian religious cultures (all those giant Buddhas and the like) now finds expression in skyscrapers, as well. Many are decorated with replicas of foreign landmarks. It's not unusual to come upon a scaled-down Tour Eiffel or Statue of Liberty topping off some enormous black shaft of an office development. Down at eye level, though, BKK (it is commonly known by its airport code) is a city of neighbour-hoods, each of them almost a tribe unto itself.

Some of these nabes are particularly associated with white foreigners. Transients have Khao San Road, which is syn-onymous with backpacks, hostels, and cheap phone cards. Expats, who are almost without exception far older than the trekkers, have Sukhumvit Road. It is the most important of five districts that shelter many thousands of Western foreigners known as *farang* (pronounced *falang*), most of them English speakers, who have fallen in love with the place or perhaps only with one of its citizens, or are enjoying a comfortable budget-retirement, or have decided for various reasons, legal, moral, or philosophical, not to return home. The Dickens of this demimonde (or maybe its Mayhew) is the aforementioned Christopher G. Moore, who has lived there several decades and, being a speaker of Thai, has learned a great deal about the workings of the host culture, as well as many secrets of the expats, most of whom are British or American. His middle initial prevents confusion with two other Christopher Moores — the American writer of trash-books read at airports and the Toronto historian and Governor General Award winner.

So far, Christopher G. has published well over twenty novels and thrillers, all of them set in Southeast Asia and most of them in Bangkok, the city that, after all, is said to have inspired *Blade Runner* and is indeed a place of fascinating sleaze and colourful crime. The concept of full disclosure compels me to confess that a small literary press I started published two of his books in the Canadian market several years ago. One of them had some favourable reviews and sold modestly well, perhaps because it opens on a grisly murder in Vancouver (where Moore once taught condo law at the University of British Columbia). The other one was not at all commercially successful in Canada, where he has never been popular the way he is in the United States, Western Europe, and Japan. Still, many Canadian readers of police-procedurals admire the books of his that feature Vincent Calvino, a disbarred New York lawyer who works as a PI in Bangkok, often in uneasy co-operation with the local cops.

Reading his books, you might expect its author to be a tough guy, but he isn't. He looks somewhat like the singer Tom Jones, is blessed with private school manners and bearing, and knows that the type of writing he does is dependent on expert listening. The last point was reinforced when, during a week's worth of bar- and restaurant-hopping, he introduced me to some of his material, on the hoof, as it were.

Sukhumvit (pronounce the *v* as a *w*), having been discovered by expats during the boom-time of the American War, is still rich in bars that are either survivors of, or tributes to, those times; joints with names that all sound like Rock 'n' Roll Texas a Go Go. In one of these, Christopher casually introduced me to an acquaintance of his who, throughout a long conversation sustained by drunken energy, was careful to keep a nervous eye on the door. A Thai woman he used to know, it seems, had hired not one but two assassins to kill him, and they meant business, too. These things happen. In another such place, where there is not only a jukebox, but one full of the timeless works of, for example, Eric Burdon and the Animals, we met a fellow who had managed to crash one of the junta-sponsored wholesale gem fairs at Mogok in northern Burma, from which Westerners, other than the few big dealers invited from Europe and elsewhere, are emphatically and indeed forcibly excluded, not just at fair-time, but year-round. Mogok owes its status as a heavily militarized forbidden-zone to the fact that it's the source of many of the world's sapphires and most of its pigeon-blood rubies, the most desirable type. The fellow was telling us the detailed story of how he not only got in, but then managed to get out again, recrossing the Thai-Burmese border, on foot this time, with one of his trouser pockets full of samples.

Smiling, being extremely courteous as always, Christopher sat, like Sebastian Flyte's teddy bear, in one corner of our booth, which was made of knotty pine. Silently, and with unblinking eye-contact, yet with an apparently effortless air of attentive distraction, as well, he was committing the entire narrative to memory, megabyte after megabyte, and turning it into a plot. The Thai bar-girl, to use her official job title, stood beneath a Budweiser sign, adjusting her vinyl miniskirt. She ignored us, as well as Gladys Knight and the Pips singing "Midnight Train to Georgia." Outside it was 93 degrees Fahrenheit. Inside it was 1968 AD.

⊰ ✳ ⊱

— HÔTEL SPLENDIDE —

In the capital of Cambodia, some months are dry and some are very wet indeed. None, however, seems substantially less hot than the others, at least not by standards upheld in the West. So the best plan, I believe, is always to stay on the eastern margin of the city, preferably along the Sisowath Quay. This is a street with only one side, for directly opposite is an embankment leading down to the waterfront. Worn steps descend to the Tonlé Sap, in the middle of which sits a large island. Along the farther shore side of the island — the back channel — is the Tonlé Mekong. These two magnificent rivers are full of life and traffic. I, for one, could gaze at them endlessly, watching all manner of river craft, from homemade fishing boats barely big enough for two people to substantial freshwater freighters, go about their business all day — and throughout the evening, as well, becoming only dots of light criss-crossing in the darkness. Yet the true advantage of being so near the water is the slight possibility of catching a breeze. One lives in hope.

The first time I visited Phnom Penh I was with M. We stayed at the Hotel Cambodiana, just down the quay, past the Royal Palace and the National Assembly. It was then a rather new joint-venture affair that was run, and very smoothly too, by people from Singapore. It was full of tourists who liked to wake in the morning not quite remembering whether they were in Phnom Penh, New York, or London. Since then, however, locals have grabbed the management contract and the establishment has declined. One evening, I decided to revisit the place for dinner. I was pleased to see that the two women from France with a pastry shop in the lobby are still there, making Gateaux Saint-Honoré (by special arrangement) and innumerable lesser desserts. But the hotel itself looked forlorn and disorganized. As I was conserving cash, I was careful to note the sticker on the door with the familiar Visa logo. Inside, at the front desk and the concierge's stand, both unmanned when I passed, were displays of Visa application forms. When I finished my meal, however, I learned that in fact the hotel no longer accepts the card. Agh!

This time, as I was making my own travel arrangements, I was staying at one of the many narrow rundown places a short walk upstream, one which, with apologies to Ludwig Bemelmans, I shall call the Hôtel Splendide, for many such establishments rejoice in grandiose names that fool no one. When I entered my room for the first time, I found a small laminated card at the spot on the pillow where, at the Cambodiana during its Singapore period, I would have expected to discover a chocolate mint. The card was certainly mint-green, but it said: NO FIREARM OPIUMS IN ROOM. My first reaction was of course to slap my forehead and exclaim "Where *are* my manners!" For local custom is evidently to check one's opiums at the front desk. Possibly this is one reason lockers are provided. The lockers look as though they might be second-hand ones from a rural bus depot.

As for the room, it had some sort of ornate plate-rail, very likely French, but the doors both interior and exterior were of lacquered plywood. The space was surprisingly clean, though while lying on the bed, I couldn't ignore enormous patches of mould that turned the ceiling into a mappa mundi. There was a narrow veranda overlooking the street. Decades of automobile particulate, however, had eaten away the stonework of the stubby balustrade. The chest of drawers and armoire had many locks, and I found a ring of keys in a desk on the opposite wall. But none of the keys matched any of the locks.

Noise from the street rose on the hot air, and at night there was a scratching sound inside one of the walls. The hot water was cold and cold drinks were warm, and there didn't seem to be enough towels or loo paper for all the rooms and no soap whatever. Nor enough cash in the till downstairs to make change for even a small purchase. When questioned about the simplest matter, staff members looked dolefully perplexed. The rest of the time they quarrelled amongst themselves, loudly and in numerous languages and dialects. The lift, which was scarcely larger than a red English telephone box, stopped at various floors randomly and closed its door quickly enough to imprison people like a Venus flytrap.

"Be thankful," said an Aussie. "This is the only thing in the whole bloody place that goes fast enough to break a sweat. But you get used to it. I've lived here sixteen years."

Later that day, when I was coming back to my room, I put the door key into the lock and the entire knob mechanism, cover plate and all, fell to the floor with a crash, leaving me with the key still in my hand. There was no one to fix the lock, so I requested another room, one with the same view. The management reluctantly agreed. And so it went.

The Quay is the Sumkumvit of Phnom Penh, but with a different sort of expat community, even though it includes many American seniors, and some Australian ones, as well, perhaps a Kiwi or two, whose principal connections to their own cultures were severed during the American War. For reasons often more psychological than strictly political, these often bitter exiles in their early or mid sixties have cast themselves out. It isn't quite accurate to say that they have, in the Australian phrase, gone troppo, for they are commonly not so well integrated into the host culture as their long residence might suggest. They are simply stubborn and defiant, frequently tired, and often a little drunk on Mekong Whisky or Angkor Beer.

Standing in contrast are the great many younger men, and, significantly, women, who arrived during or after the genocidal civil wars, often working for government aid agencies and NGOs of one sort or another. This group includes a large segment of francophones. Thus the Phnom Penh scene is again set apart from Bangkok's. There is no historical reason for French to be spoken in Thailand, the only country in the region that has never been officially a Western or Japanese colony. In many other ways too, the old-timers, the ones that is who still have lives and livers, share little with the new breed, who are well educated and well paid. It's for these latter folks, as well as the tourists, that streets like the Quay are lined with intimate bars and bistros, and restos selling premium fair-trade coffees rather than Nescafé.

Only a short distance along the Quay from the Splendide is a hotel called the Indochine, though it's obviously run by Aussies, as the logo is a kangaroo. Another neighbour is a former ship chandler who now repairs and rebuilds motorcycles — motos. They are found everywhere. The current custom, as two different people explained to me, is for parents to buy their son a moto so he can commute to school. Many of the young men, however, sell them to such a person as the shop owner and use the money to gamble on soccer matches. Gambling is one of the few traditional vices legal in Cambodia, as distinct from all the others, which go on without much regard for the law one way or the other; there even used to be a large floating casino opposite the Royal Palace. Of the remaining addresses in my section of the Quay, many were taken up with ambiguous massage places, mini-marts, money changers, and shops selling pirated DVDs of movies. Other than these, and the open-air work space and showroom of a maker of sometimes rather kitschy coffins, virtually every other shophouse is a cellphone place, so many of them that surely the market penetration must be total. I've always felt that allowing the military to own businesses, making the generals and the colonels no longer quite so dependent on the government for funding, is a terrible mistake. Just as one of the biggest savings and lending institutions in Bangkok is the Thai Military Bank, so one of the biggest phone companies in Cambodia is owned by the army.

Still, for all the French tourists and public-policy workers, one must squint one's ears to hear French spoken recklessly in the streets of Phnom Penh (in the boulevard Mao Tsé-Toung, *par exemple*), so great is the general babble. The French wish is to cling to whatever influence they retain while not appearing to be interested in political or even economic power. Sometimes one will see or meet someone from the French embassy, which, significantly perhaps, is, of the all the legations in the capital, the one located farthest from the urban centre of action.

One of the shops selling the pirated movies boasted a sign announcing that it has a selection of films in French. On inspection I discovered that the inventory inclines heavily toward *La Déchirure*, *La Soupe au canard* and *Indochine* — that is, *The Killing Fields* avec Sam Waterston, *Duck Soup* avec Groucho Marx, and, well, *Indochine* avec Catherine Deneuve. The above titles no doubt symbolize once again the pointlessness of my making this journey, not only for its own sake, but also to gauge the amount of lingering French in the region — and to return imaginatively to the era of the postcards, trying to understand something of the people snapping the shutter, as well as of those being photographed.

Just as the presence of the *Bangkok Post* and the *Nation* show the strength of the English language in Thailand, the newspapers in Phnom Penh show the comparative poverty of French in Cambodia. The *Phnom Penh Post*, published only in English as the name suggests, is far and away the most important foreign newspaper in the country. It dares to report Cambodian politics honestly despite fierce government suspicion. Perhaps its most closely read feature, however, is the always lively Police Blotter, from which I cannot help but quote at random for the insight it gives on the city's daily life.

> Police on Thursday raided a café showing porn movies in Chamkarmon district, Phnom Penh, arresting 100 including the café's two female owners. Police seized 74 motorbikes and the equipment used for showing movies. All but the owners were later released with their motorbikes, but they had to pay money to the police for various reasons.

You will find nothing so sociologically revealing in the *Cambodia Daily*, which is some sort of subsidized training ground for tyro journalists and looks as though it's been produced at Kinko's. It is far below the level of the *Cambodia Weekly*, published by the University of Cambodia. That leaves only *Cambodge Soir Hebdo*, which, though it ventures into current affairs, does so cautiously. I saw a headline — LES ROYALISTES À NOUVEAU PLONGÉS DANS LE CHAOS — that might have been plucked from the time the postcards were printed. But then the paper is not independent, but rather *"est soutenu par l'Organisation internationale de la francophonie."*

Buildings outlive persons, especially in places where economic growth was slow for so many decades and health care remains, to put the best possible face on the situation, rather basic. Despite the rush of development between the end of the civil war era in 1999 and the global economic crisis a decade later, Phnom Penh certainly harbours examples of French colonial architecture. The quickest to be preserved are the private residences, which are called villas even though they're in the centre of the city, far from the countryside. They are customarily two storeys high with an elaborate central entranceway and tall, narrow windows with louvered wooden shutters, the whole affair surrounded by a wall (protective but also decorative). The exteriors are often pastel — yellows or blues — and the roofs have Asian lines. These were the homes of French merchants and businessmen, and they appear not to have changed much over the years. Some were pointed out to me as late nineteenth century and at least one as being from the 1930s. The only example I saw that was dated had *1926* in a cartouche over the upper storey. Did these people know how quickly their empire there would vanish once the Second World War cleared the ground for fierce nativism to grow?

Some French buildings on the grander scale, which is to say ones perhaps too big for a single foreign individual to purchase, repair, and restore, have fared far less well. One of these, the former Hôtel Renaske, stands vacant and has been the subject of various legal actions; it may meet the fate of so many smaller ones and be torn down or permitted to collapse. Another one, near the palace, is a wonderfully and monumentally bizarre two-storey mansion with large porticos. It has ornate masonry work everywhere. Although it juggles allegorical Khmer motifs with its many Corinthian columns, it is most definitely the work of a European sensibility. It is also a ruin. The wall and gate are shot up and cracking. The windows are knocked out, a few boarded over with plywood or corrugated iron, but most not. Old tires and wrecked automobiles litter the front garden, which is overgrown with weeds. Birds and animals nest in the arches and on the ledges. Trees grow inside the building itself; one of them is tall enough to be visible through a formerly ornate second-storey window.

I asked Vorn, a young character I had retained for his Local Knowledge, what had befallen this marvellous pile of stones.

"The King build for bodyguards," he explained. "No more King."

"But still plenty of bodyguards, eh?" I repied.

Cambodia, like the former Soviet Union, found that as soon as it loosened control of the economy it gained, overnight, a mafia class, whose members enjoyed driving round the city with all their heavily armed retainers, some of them non-Asians, big fellows, Russian perhaps.

Vorn shrugged.

Later I learned that the building is not entirely without some civic purpose. From time to time, it seems, rock concerts have been held there. That may account for some of the outright damage just as the withering of royalist sentiment explains some of the mere neglect. But who knows? The country has gone through such hell in the past few decades that any survival seems miraculous and any loss perfectly if tragically predictable.

The pollution in Phnom Penh, no doubt combined with that of Bangkok, soon left me with a lung ailment. I was able to go to the Russian Market and buy 400 milligrams of Noroxin without a prescription — after carefully checking to see that it hadn't exceeded its best-before date and showed no evidence of being counterfeit. One doesn't require a doctor's scrip in Cambodia because there are too few doctors. Historically speaking, the shortage goes back to the Pol Pot regime, when most of licensed professionals who didn't flee were systematically murdered. In Thailand by comparison, one needs only a quick nod from a medical middle-man to obtain whatever prescription one seeks. I'm told that the system helps to prevent an even faster spread of sexually transmitted diseases. Lord knows what sort of treatment is available to the sex workers and johns of Kilometre Eleven, the horrifying prostitution-village that sprang up eleven kilometres outside Phnom Penh, catering originally to UN peacekeepers.

⊰ ✸ ⊱

— TELEGRAMS FROM ANGKOR WAT —

Vorn is still a young man. I never asked his age, but he was in his twenties when I first met him a few years ago.

M and I were travelling together.

"How many sons you have?" he asked M, whom I had briefed on the rigours of Southeast Asian etiquette.

"No sons," she said, smiling.

"Girls?" he said without contempt, as he prides himself on the sensitive understanding of Western culture he has gained through being what once upon a time, in China, would have been called a comprador, a Portuguese word: adviser, translator, and, most important of all, fixer.

"No girls, either."

He then turned to me and said accusingly, "You never worked enough!"

M and I had just returned from a wild boat trip under the guidance of one of Vorn's brothers-in-law or cousins. These are almost without number. Whatever item or service one needs, whatever deal one is looking for in fields as different as consumer electronics, physiotherapy or the foreign-exchange market, he knows the ideal person, a relative by marriage if not by blood, located, as luck would have it, only moments away.

The boat-operator looked nothing whatever like Vorn, but spoke of him warmly, as far as we could tell. We were in a long-tail boat at the southern end of Tonlé Sap. This is to say, the largest lake in Southeast Asia by far. It becomes still larger during the summer wet season when we were there, going from an area of about 2,500 square kilometres to at least thirteen thousand, inundating the surrounding forests and reversing the flow of Tonlé Sap, the river of the same name, testing the very safety of the elaborate dikes at Phnom Penh, two hundred or so kilometres away. The lake supplies fish to the majority of Cambodia's people.

The lake is a spooky place when in flood. With the motor off, we sat holding onto the gunnels, rocking in the thick of a forest that the sun barely penetrates. Or rather the top half of the forest, the rest being underwater for the next few months. We carefully tiptoed, so to speak, into the open water, where the lapping sound has the power both to put people to sleep or drive them mad. There were no other sounds, in fact, no other signs of life. The water and the sky were grey. But retreating into the mouth of the river, travelling down the river that usually runs up, there was humanity everywhere: men building a large wooden vessel along the bank using only hand tools, children swimming naked, people stepping gingerly from one flat-bottom boat to the next. On the lake itself, there is one entire floating city of about ten thousand people who rarely, if ever, set foot on land and have no reason to.

As we proceeded slowly to where Vorn waited in the second-hand car of which he was so proud, we peered into all the bamboo baskets full of fish, meat, and vegetables along the way and stopped to go aboard a barge that served as a weird sort of floating zoo. It contained, among other creatures, some type of aggressive lizard I had never seen before, rather more than a metre long. It responded with a fierce lunge when I tapped gently on the bars of its cage. Farther along, some enormously ugly birds were sitting atop old pilings driven into the mud and the pitched ends of thatched-roof dwellings. From a distance, I thought they were vultures, though they were much too big. No, they were storks. They looked like soldiers guarding a train. Only their eyes moved, rather too suspiciously, it seemed to me.

Tonlé Sap is one of two sites that Cambodians enjoy showing off to Western visitors. The main one, of course, is Angkor, the temple complex that is the hearthstone of Khmer culture. The civilization was at its rather troubled zenith when the structures were being built, between the ninth and the fourteenth centuries CE. It once stretched northward into the lower reaches of China and both eastward and westward into what are now Vietnam and Thailand respectively. Such incursions into neighbouring cultures were of course reciprocated. Siem Reap, the city one must go to in order to access Angkor, is sometimes translated as "raped by the Siamese."

If not a *deeply* spiritual person, I am certainly not an unspiritual one, but in any case am in no position to explain or pass judgment on the magnetic attraction Angkor holds for the West's many time-share Buddhists and similar faddists. They swarm over the site season after season, many of them staying weeks at a time, making complete circuits of the intricate but often fragile carvings that decorate individual walls and buildings. Certainly Angkor is an architectural and archaeological marvel, comparable on those scores to Bagan in Burma and Borobudur in Indonesia, which are much less famous in the world at large. (I'm not embarrassed to say that I first became aware of Angkor from the poem "Angkor Wat" written by Allen Ginsberg in 1963.)

Here I could interject a capsule history of Angkor, having digested the relevant books, but I would risk boring readers until they sobbed. Instead I'll quote, with her permission, from M's telegraphic notebook entries about the bas-relief stone carvings, for her memory-prompts are all the more vivid for being so impressionistic. She writes:

> Angkor Thom [building] — snake monument gates, elephants!, earthworks surrounding.

> East side — bas-reliefs at entrance, Chinese soldiers, banners and parasols, cockfighting!, tortoise eats man!

South side — elephant troops, horse troops, ground troops, boat soldiers. Man falls off boat, crocodile eats him. Men hunting tigers.

Daily life in Cambodia — baskets for vegetables, picking lice from hair (especially after harvest), Jayavarman VII built 102 hospitals for all people, birth scene, Khmers v Chinese, wild boar fighting, Khmer wrestling (with helmets), Cham v Khmer (ground battle).

Celebration — grill meat, carry pig. Quarry work 42 km from here …

And later, in another part of the site, a structure called

The Terrace of the Elephants. Had a roof of tile & wood. Received groups of people (VIPs waiting for king).

Families came to see — Victory Road, Victory Gate.

[Then the famous Angkor Wat itself] New Year's celebrations here, dance, 12 towers. Elephants carrying tree trunks.

Filmed here few years ago: *Lara Croft: Tomb Raider*, Angelina Jolie.

W.C. 500 riels. (4,000 riels = $US1).

The most blatant example of colonialist and Orientalist thinking is to say that Angkor was discovered by the French, for of course it had never been misplaced much less lost. It hadn't even been abandoned, not permanently. Nor were the French the first outsiders on the scene. Portuguese travellers saw it in the sixteenth century, Japanese in the seventeenth. After spending two days at Angkor, a French missionary, Father Charles-Émile Bouillevaux, wrote about its wonders in *Ma visite aux ruines cambodgiennes en 1850* without attracting the world's attention. That was left to the resolute French botanist and explorer Henri Mouhot (1826–61). So evocative was his prose in *Voyage dans les royaumes de Siam, de Cambodge, de Laos et autres parties de l'Indochine*, and so fascinating its illustrations, that a great vogue for Angkor developed in Europe and Britain, an excitement kept on the boil by the work of Francis Garnier and others. Mouhot's book was published seven years after his death from a fever near Luang Prabang, following the fourth of his expeditions, all of them marked by terrible suffering and hardship.

Unlike many who followed, Mouhot was a scientist who seems to have been without serious political or commercial ambitions. Yet his work came at the right moment to dovetail with France's construction of its Indochinese empire. It also, whether consciously or not, advanced the notion of Indochina as exotic — romantic, enticing, and dangerous, a region of strange cultures and forbidden customs. A place, in other words, that had much in common with French possessions in North Africa, the South Pacific, and elsewhere, at least in the minds of their European masters. Gauguin might easily have done what he did in Indochina rather than Polynesia. Artists and intellectuals in particular continued to fall for such thinking decade after decade. Consider André Malraux.

In 1923, the intense young literary johnny went out to Cambodia to make his fortune, having already squandered the one that came with his first wife. He had always been able to earn a little extra money in the art galleries and auction rooms of Paris as a commission-based go-between linking artists and collectors. Now he resolved to become his own supplier. He knew that a certain type of statuette of a Buddhist apsara, for example, could bring twelve thousand American dollars in New York. So he and a colleague, posing as serious archaeologists, went to the ruins of Banteay Srei, northeast of Angkor, and pried loose seven sandstone bas-reliefs.

French intelligence agencies were already on to him (just as their British and American opposite numbers would be in subsequent years). He was arrested, tried, and sentenced to three years. Back in Europe, his wife orchestrated a campaign of getting leading intellectual figures to petition for his release. Surprisingly, the effort was successful. A couple of years later, Malraux returned to the colonies to start a pro-independence newspaper called *L'Indochine*, which the French authorities closed down. Out of his temple-robbing experiences came his famous novel *La voie royale* (1930).

The other side of the coin was that Paris became the world centre of genuine scholarship about Indochina, just as London became so with respect to the parts of the world it was colonizing. Cambodia, Laos, and Vietnam owe much to France's intellectual institutions. European colonialism, already such a complex and often contradictory proposition, was complicated still further by cultural differences that distinguished one colonizing power from another within their common goal of making money. What was the first project undertaken by foreign masters when imposing their authority over a new place? The Chinese would build a market, the Americans a gaol, the Spanish a cathedral, the British a library, and the French an opera house. This statement, of course, is not in the least scientific, but only the accurate recounting of what a wise-cracker might suppose while travelling.

※

— THE HORROR —

In 1970, François Bizot, a French ethnologist with five years' Cambodian experience, was restoring ceramics and bronzes when he learned that heavy fighting had broken out in Siem Reap. A civil war had begun. The Americans in Vietnam had recently backed a coup against the Cambodian king. They installed as the new ruler a favourite general, Lon Nol, who was now on the rampage against communists, both the domestic Khmers Rouges and the neighbouring Vietnamese. A prudent ethnologist would have got the hell out. Bizot, however, remained in-country and came to grief in the following year.

"My work had taken me to a monastery in the Oudong area, to the west of Phnom Penh, [to conduct] research into Buddhist practices associated with the state of trance," he would write in an important memoir entitled *Le Portail*. "We were due to visit an elderly monk who was known for his knowledge of rites. When we arrived, we were ambushed by a group of Khmers Rouges. I recognised their uniforms, imitating the trousers and black shirts of peasants." They thought he was a spy working for the CIA. In fact, he was demonstrably anti-American. "Whenever a Khmer spoke to me in English, it put me in a bad mood straight away," he wrote. The language reminded him of "the Americans' uncouth methods, their crass ignorance of the milieu in which they had intervened, their clumsy demagogy, their misplaced clear conscience, and that easygoing, childlike sincerity that bordered on foolishness. They were total strangers in the area, driven by clichés."

Bizot was force-marched to a jungle camp whose other prisoners were to be murdered one by one, usually by being bludgeoned with a tree branch or a spade. He quickly met the man named Kang Kech Leu (one Chinese parent, you see) but called Ta Duch (the honorific means "grandfather," but has nothing to do with age). Duch, spelled Douch by the French, was a former mathematics teacher with "a friendly air" and unprepossessing style. "His black jacket was too big and his trousers stopped just above the ankle, revealing finely shaped feet [...] He looked young, not yet 30. Nothing in his unassuming demeanour had indicated to me that he was in charge here. But his authority was total; there were no limits to his power over the detainees."

Bizot managed to survive because Duch and he became friends. They respected each other and every day had intellectualized and even philosophical conversations. Bizot wasn't a victim of Stockholm Syndrome, for he did not embrace any of Duch's precepts or beliefs. He simply found him fascinating, "a child venturing among wolves: to survive, he had drunk their milk, and learned how to howl like them, and let instinct take over." Elsewhere, Bizot writes: "somehow I trusted him. Of course he would have me killed without hesitation if the order came [yet this] terrible man was not duplicitous; all he had were principles and convictions."

Such was the friendship that Bizot, a fluent Khmer speaker, realized over time that Duch was willing to buck the chain of command to get his favourite captive released after only a few months. When challenged at one level, Duch went higher up, until he got the order to let Bizot go. The order was ultimately confirmed by the despotic and genocidal Pol Pot himself. In Bizot's telling, such tactics put Duch in line for praise as well as putting him at risk. "My freedom, obtained after a hard struggle, had become a sort of personal success for him, spurring on his career as a revolutionary." On Bizot's last day in custody, Duch threw him an all-night farewell party attended by all the other inmates, who would be killed soon afterwards. The relationship of the two men sounds like something from a Graham Greene novel, not because of the tropical locale or the wartime setting, but rather because of the twisted moral atmosphere in which two such figures could become buddies.

In 1975, at the same moment the Americans were driven out of Saigon, the Khmer Rouge, the extremely radical and merciless agrarian movement led by Pol Pot, became the government of Cambodia by storming into Phnom Penh unopposed, forcing the populace to vacate the city for the countryside. Phnom Penh was soon a ghost town. Pol Pot also tried to eliminate religion, family relationships, money, and even the very concept of time (calendars and clocks were forbidden). He murdered not merely ethnic minorities, but whole classes of society. Teachers, students, administrators, and anyone considered an "intellectual" ended up in a shallow grave. Even those who merely *looked* as though they might be educated were exterminated. For example, people with little depressions on the bridge of the nose suggesting that they wore spectacles and therefore knew how to read and thus were subversives. He killed many types of peasant farmer, as well. Pol Pot's Cambodia was one of the twentieth century's notable dystopian nightmares, yet he believed himself an idealist.

Years after his release and the horrors that followed the horror of the civil war itself, Bizot returned to Cambodia where he learned that Duch, following his assignment at the prison camp, became a major executioner (the shuddering irony that Greene would have loved). He became in fact the commandant of the former high school known as S-21. This was the secret prison used as a holding area for prisoners later sent to execution by the truckload. It was discovered by the invading Vietnamese soldiers in 1979. Between fourteen thousand and sixteen thousand prisoners, including many murdered on the spot and hastily buried out back, spent their last days there. It is a moving and horrifying place. When M and I went there a few years ago, we were shown around by a man who became quite emotional as the tour went on. He spoke faster and faster until his tenuous grasp of English began to slip, so that Pol Pot's name came out sounding, to our ears at least, like *purple*. Finally he told us of all the members of his family who had been murdered there.

Pol Pot died in 1998, but Khmer Rouge elements still participate in governing Cambodia. This fact has made a mockery of the deal the United Nations reached with Cambodia in 2003 to finally put some highly placed former Khmer Rouge officials on trial, cases that would be heard in Cambodian courts and financed through private donations. So great was the reluctance to bring imprisoned Khmer Rouge leaders to justice that a number of them died off in the interim. Duch, however, was a healthy sixty-six when I returned to Phnom Penh in 2009. The day I checked into the Hôtel Splendide was also the first day of his trial. The city was full of foreign reporters from Agence-France Presse and the West's other large media organizations. When his turn came to make an opening statement, Duch apologized. Not everyone took his sincerity seriously, but then he could hardly stand in the docket and say "It wasn't me, it was some other dog." Contemplating Duch, one cannot help but remember Hannah Arendt's famous statement about "the banality of evil" in her book about the Nazi war criminal Adolf Eichmann.

For his part, Bizot remains an interesting character: mysterious and elusive and evidently more of an ideologue than his captor. He has written of how the Americans' "irresponsibility, their colossal tactlessness, their inexcusable naïveté, even their cynicism, frequently aroused more fury and outrage in me than did the lies of the communists." This passage has been much quoted in France, where his book became a bestseller, and in the United States, where people puzzle that someone can be both anti-communist and anti-American.

⚜ ✳ ⚛

— A BISTRO TALE —

Japan's stated aim in the 1930s was to drive Westerners out of coastal Asia, north as well as south (so they could have it all to themselves); the name they gave this grand design was the Asia Co-Prosperity Sphere. Once they had been defeated in the Second World War, they saw the remarkable extent that expansionism based on dislike of Westerners survived in other people's hands under another banner: independence. In country after country, such Asian nationalism ended the Europeans' colonial rule from the later 1940s through the 1960s. The West reclaimed the territories that Japan had overrun, but would lose them again, permanently this time, to ideologies far removed from Japanese fascism. The British relinquished India, of course, but also Burma, Singapore, and Malaya, just as the Dutch were forced to give up Indonesia and the French, Indochina.

In Southeast Asia, just as everywhere else, race always has been an important element in the way societies are organized. So it is that today Cambodia, like its neighbours, doesn't display much affection for the Western workers, expats, and visitors who reside there. It only tolerates them for what's in their pockets. As is also the case in Vietnam and Laos, foreigners aren't permitted to own real property, no matter how long they've lived there (whereas Thailand, slightly more liberal, allows Caucasians to own condos but not houses).

I was disappointed to learn that Cambodia's rattletrap system of passenger trains, which often broke down temporarily en route, finally did so permanently. Now only freight is carried, very very slowly, on the rapidly deteriorating right-of-way. This was inconvenient news because I wished to get out of Phnom Penh for a couple of days and go to Battambang, to the northwest, where I was told there was a concentration of old French buildings less deformed by the needs of commerce than those in the capital. Some maps show a small airport at Battambang, but they are incorrect. There is, however, a bus service. Compared with the train, which used to take eighteen hours or so, the bus requires only eight or nine hours, but is, people warned me, quite uncomfortable. For example, it had air conditioning with only one setting — full blast — but no toilet, and I was told that it was unlikely that I would meet anyone I could communicate with. So there was no question of what to do: I borrowed somebody's mobile and phoned Vorn. He reminded me of those hard-boiled private eyes of the old pulp magazines who got twenty-five dollars a day and expenses. Only in his case, the rate was fifteen dollars a day and petrol. For him, this was not too bad a deal. Cambodia's per capita income is US$500 per annum.

I was to meet him shortly after first light at a bistro called L'Oiseau Rouge. It was a bistro in the classic European sense, a nice dark bar with a small stage and a grill that was kept hot all night. I was off in a corner by myself, carbo-loading on breakfast to see me through the long day. There were three Khmer women, one in her thirties, obviously the manager, and two very young ones, attending to various things behind the bar. There was only one other customer, an immense Australian fellow sitting at the bar with his back to me. He had red hair stored in a ponytail and was wearing a loud tropical shirt and khaki trousers. His feet, resting on the rung of the barstool, were bare. Sometime during the night, which he had obviously spent relentlessly drinking, he had kicked off his shoes and let them drop to the floor. He was still ordering drinks. Why he hadn't been cut off, I couldn't imagine — except that he was dutifully paying for them and also of course because without them he might have erupted in genuine violence.

There was enough material in his hideous shirt to sail a square-rigged ship. He weighed, I would guess, 120 kilos, and he was very loud and getting louder. He kept yelling Aussie endearments to the women. This was followed by reaching across the bar as far as he could stretch to grab their bottoms or grope their breasts, whichever were closer. I had a wide-angle view of all this as I sat unnoticed, peering over the top of my newspaper.

Hearing the rumpus, the night security guard appeared out of nowhere. A Khmer fellow, quite small and slight, he surveyed the situation and sensibly decided to take his lunch break early. *This isn't going to end well*, I said to myself. But fortunately I was wrong. Once the customer had finished his current drink, the headwoman came out from behind the bar and, using a normal conversational tone, engaged him in chat while she slipped behind him and began giving him a shoulder massage. After five or ten minutes, he crossed his arms on the bar and rested his head in the cradle they made. A few more moments and he was sound asleep.

Of all the ways such a situation might have concluded, this was not one I had imagined. I was recounting the story to Vorn as soon as he scooped me up in his car and we set off through the still largely deserted streets. I explained what had happened, using carefully deliberate sentences, for I had noticed that his English comprehension was diminished when he was having to concentrate on the road. When I finished, he replied: "Man stay sleep when you leave. They take his money then."

⊰ ✳ ⊱

George Fetherling

— GOING TO MARKET —

It was thoroughly daylight as we made our way through the seedier streets of Phnom Penh, past the container port, through the bleak and resentful Muslim section where a group of men were at prayer in an open-fronted mosque and women tended small fires in the dirty lanes to dispose of the family rubbish. Eventually, the city just sort of gave out, as though in defeat, and we were plunged into a ragtag industrial area that was waking up to the day's business.

The proof of this were the motos that had little square trailers hitched to them. Sheets of wood had been laid across the beds of the trailers. These platforms supported young people, girls and women mostly, as many as thirty or forty either standing or squatting or sitting with their legs dangling over the sides. It seems impossible that so many bodies could fit on such a small surface or that one tiny engine could pull so much weight. These were workers going to begin their day in one factory or another and they were illustrative not just of a new generation's promise, but of a problem, as well.

So many of the social ills in Asian countries are a result of the way cities have been flooded by people leaving their homes in towns and the countryside to find work. For example, Bangkok has 10 or maybe 12 million people while the next-largest Thai centre, Chiang Mai, has only about three hundred thousand. Phnom Penh certainly has a million residents; the total may be nearer 2 million. But Battambang, the second-biggest community in Cambodia, is home to perhaps 150,000. The people we kept passing were rural folks seeking a better life, but being dragged to exploitative dead-end jobs where long days of brutally repetitive labour might, or might not, provide a little money to send back to their families.

We entered Kampong Chhnang province. The name translates roughly as "pottery port," for the area is synonymous with a certain type of brown clay vessel. Thousands of examples from the smallest to the most huge were stacked up along the highway to tempt customers. Except for long, completely rural, stretches between villages and towns, there was always activity along the shoulders. Nearly every house, however humble, had some sort of little unpainted stand by the road with a few vegetables or soft drinks for sale. Men fixed motos by the berm while women hawked religious articles and general kitsch. I avoided the temptation to read too much significance into the little braziers where people bought frog meat, cut into strips and grilled with a sauce I couldn't identify and Vorn didn't know the English word for. Yes, in an earlier age of ignorance many bigoted Anglos referred to French people as "Frogs." The slur derived from the fact that frog legs were often listed on menus in France. But I doubt very much that the French enthusiasm for that delicacy was transferred to its Cambodian colony. Cambodia simply has a great many frogs: rather large ones, it appears. So does Vietnam. In both places, they are eaten by ordinary folks. They aren't expensive, aren't elaborately prepared, and aren't considered a gourmet treat. I wasn't finding much of a French presence in the former French Indochina, but I was trying not to reach too far for it, either.

The actual town of Kampong Chhnang may seem the type of place where nothing ever appears to happen, but it does afford something to travellers interested in twentieth-century history. Comparisons between some rundown French houses and Khmer dwellings on stilts give another hint of how life was lived by the people on different sides of the camera lens. Then there is a completely unsubtle reminder of a more recent past. Just outside town are the overgrown ruins of a large airport engineered and financed by the Chinese during the Khmer Rouge regime, supposedly for peaceful domestic uses, but perhaps also, as is widely believed, as a base for the Cambodians to attack the Vietnamese (who instead attacked them). The runway was built by corvée labourers. Once the job was done, Pol Pot is said to have had all of them murdered.

The heat made the road appear to shimmer. It was about noon. The only significant place before we reached Battambang would be Pursat, capital of the province of the same name. The place had more traffic than Kampong Chhnang and seemed a bit livelier, but that may have been my thirst and hunger talking. Here, too, there were colonial-era buildings put to postcolonial uses, but shown no respect. I suggested we stop there for a cool drink and a bite to eat, but Vorn was determined to push on. In time, his reasoning became clear. Not far beyond the city was a restaurant he knew, one operated, I presumed, by a putative grandparent, cousin, in-law, aunt, or uncle. I wasn't certain which, but whoever was in charge welcomed him fulsomely and seemed willing to tolerate me. The few tables were outdoors, under a plastic canopy. They provided shade for the spike-haired dogs that, between alms from the humans, slept beneath the tables. Fruit flies buzzed all round. There was no menu. Vorn simply exchanged a word or two with his cherished family member and a teenage girl wearing a traditional skirt and a Planet Hollywood T-shirt brought each of us a bowl and a tiny plate. I thought I had eaten most every type of East Asian cuisine, in circumstances ranging from streets stalls to formal banquets. But rice was the only dish I recognized here.

Throughout the meal, Vorn seemed to be looking at me oddly. At first I thought he was watching the movement of my mouth, the way a lip-reader would, for he and I both found that we understood each other better when we were speaking face-to-face and were concentrating on what we were hearing. Or maybe I had dropped a bite of food. Perhaps I had a dollop of *bobor* in the corner of my mouth or a spot of *samla* on the collar of my brand-new fatigues (the indestructible type known to Canadians as Tilleys, after their Vancouver manufacturer). Soon he stepped out and walked toward the road where mobile-phone reception was evidently better. I watched the pantomime of him making several calls. I presumed he was arranging our next stop — possibly at some dilapidated guest house in Battambang, run by another imaginary family member, where he would receive yet another kickback. Suddenly he snapped shut the jaw of his phone and we were off down the road once again.

At length, we did indeed make it to Battambang, capital of the next province along, an old community, but one that hasn't been part of Cambodia for very long — not in historical terms. Starting in the fifteenth century and for much of its existence thereafter, it was fought over by the Siamese, the Burmese, the Vietnamese, the Chinese, and, in a nasty series of civil wars, by the Khmers themselves. The first of these groups, the Thais, proved the longest-lived rulers. For more than a century, from 1795 to 1907, the title of lord protector, the name given to the overlord appointed by the Thais, was held by successive members of a single family. It was during the latter half of this period that the French, who already had the other part of modern Cambodia in their shopping basket, were scheming and finagling to get control of this area, as well. Among the advantages they saw there were the riches of Chuor Phnom Kravanh — the Cardamom Mountains. This range is the primary source of cardamom, a plant that is a relative of the ginger and whose black seeds are a herbal medicine as well as a spice. In the olden days, cardamom merchants from France — plump bearded men wearing white linen suits and *sola topis* — would turn up each year to bargain for the harvest and arrange for its shipment to Europe.

However difficult life was for the Khmers under the French, it was better than life under the Thais had been. There was a suffocating caste system somewhat like that of India, but in one sense worse. *Khnhom* or slaves comprised a large segment of society and their children became slaves, as well. Most were debtors, captured enemy soldiers or petty criminals. The fate of those in the third category easily might have been worse. Painful, degrading, and often hideous punishments were selected from an extensive menu. In those days before the French introduced the non-judgmental guillotine, prisoners, each wearing a red flower in his hair, were executed, sometimes extrajudicially, by an official who first bound them in front of an open pit and then performed an elaborate circular dance before decapitating them. Rules forbade a prisoner to be killed all by himself; the victims were always dispatched in pairs. The executioner's weapon was a sword called *srey khmav*: the Black Lady. It was the personal property of the lord governor.

The lords governor owned all the rice fields, as well. They collected confiscatory taxes on the people who worked them and also on those who picked the cardamom seeds (thus igniting the Cardamom Rebellion of 1898, the only uprising against Thai rule). The last of the line of lords governor was said to possess an ice machine; everyone else did without this valuable commodity. The middle and lower classes lived on crocodile meat, fish, and vegetables. They got along mostly by means of subsistence farming and a few crafts. For example, they made both paper fans and gunpowder. For the latter, they used saltpetre they mined themselves, but the finished product was of such poor quality that it could be used only for cheap fireworks. Travel was often by elephant or buffalo. (When the French took over in 1907, they found that only four people in the province owned bicycles.) This particular bit of Indochina was in surprising ways both less Indian and less Chinese than one might expect. Battambang was a society without, for example, restaurants, tailors or barbers, though it was one that was avid for cockfighting and particularly rich in odd folk beliefs. When first the French administration and then the Catholic Church established hospitals in Battambang, the Khmers boycotted them on superstitious grounds.

A crude census taken in 1884 by the French, who were well on their way to supplanting the Thais through a policy of exploiting the complex ethnic animosities and wars, recorded six thousand Chinese in the province out of a total population of more than a hundred thousand. There were also Vietnamese, Burmese, Lao, and Javanese people, but surprisingly few actual Thais, only about eight hundred. Among the dominant Khmer population, however, were twenty thousand "Khmer who claim to be Thai." Thais got control again, from 1941 to 1946, when the French temporarily lost the colonies to the Japanese.

Battambang today is much less interesting than the above might lead you to expect. One drives into town past an enormously long wall that supports a contemporary sculpture, donated by an admirer in California, in which scores of male figures in a line are holding a mammoth cobra: a retelling of the snake goddess legend. Then one crosses over the Sangker (also known, more quaintly, as the Sângkê), a river that, like numerous others in Cambodia, has been canalized as a flood-control measure. Then it's right into the centre of the city where some of the large public buildings, such as the Commissariat de la police, are shabby and poor-looking. The best preserved is the former French governor's mansion, painted the same shade of yellow one sees on old official buildings in this part of the world wherever the Tricolour once flew. There is a museum in town, open again after a long closure, and accessible by pounding on the massive metal doors suggesting the gates of a castle. It's a tiny place given over to early Khmer carvings and other artworks, labelled in French in the most basic, and, well, primitive way in terms of museumology. Three or four staff sat at one end of the single room, playing cards and gossiping in low tones appropriate to the august surroundings. The place smells like a tomb.

In sharp contrast to Siem Reap, as little as three or four hours away by fast boat, depending on the stage of the river, Battambang has few foreigners. I saw none, in fact. This was a far cry from a decade or so ago when United Nations troops and bureaucrats were there. For Battambang is a market town, pure and simple. Certainly the multi-storey indoor/outdoor market is the scene of whatever activity exists. It squats, tumbling down slowly, in a large square, round which young people, desperate with the boredom of small-town youth, race their motos while yakking on their mobiles. At one end of the market is an art deco clock tower of four or five storeys; the clock mechanism itself was removed years ago, so that the only way one could determine the time of day would be by using the tower as a sundial. At ground level, three generations of women, who seem to be given spots in the shade on the basis of their seniority, haggle with potential customers over the price of vegetables. Just as so many markets in Europe or America once did, this one has a small and utterly unprepossessing hotel nearby (Hotel Paris Hotel — a Chinese establishment) to serve the needs of farmers who have travelled some distance to sell their produce.

I heard no French, indeed saw no French on signs or in newspapers. The old story I have heard so often all over Asia grows inexorably truer with time: English, English of a kind at least, is becoming the second language (though the future probably favours Mandarin instead). A few years ago one might have expected "Gecko Café — Good food, drinks & foot massage" to signify an expat establishment. But not necessarily any longer, or at least not here. It was full of Khmer youth who are encouraged to drive their motos right up to the bar. Along the river there are still old shophouses from the French period, many of them decayed, one burned, a large number of them functioning as mobile phone shops. In the market I found one shophouse with a stepped roof, like a house in Amsterdam. It can only have been built by someone from northern France. Otherwise, as far as my ears could detect, there was only the sound of the wind erasing the faint traces of European colonialism.

꙳ ✳ ꙳

— DIPLOMACY —

The following day, as we were driving back to Phnom Penh, I could tell that Vorn was up to something, but I couldn't tell what. Finally, not more than an hour away from the metropolis, he let it slip with perfect timing. Permit me to summarize what was in fact a long conversation often interrupted by honking at water buffalo and other drivers.

When all of Cambodia's cumulative military troubles — Americans, rebels, Pol Pot, Vietnamese, peacekeepers — finally subsided, the country was left with an enormous stock-pile of small arms and ammunition, tonne upon tonne of the stuff, cached or abandoned and turning up everywhere. If properly stored, ammunition can have a very long life before becoming unstable. Clever businessmen, testing entrepre-neurial instincts that had lain dormant during long years of totally state-driven economics, started buying up the stuff and opening shooting galleries. This coincided with the rise in Western tourism. Visitors would go to these target ranges and exercise their adrenal glands by firing rifles and machine guns until the cows came home. No handguns, mind you, only shoulder weapons. High-end customers, however, were sometimes allowed to fire small rockets. At one such estab-lishment, those wishing a truly special holiday memory to take with them back to the States were shown how to throw hand grenades.

At length, all this became too much for the government, which began cracking down amid calls for more calm in the society generally. This was the stage, for example, at which, in a development frequently mentioned even now, banks began forbidding customers to carry automatic weapons onto bank property lest their motive be misunderstood by staff and fellow patrons. The result was that only one shooting range remained and it was part of the government, which profited from it just as the private sector had done when competition was fierce. The range was located at an army training camp where, in a dazzling coincidence, Vorn's uncle was in charge. Vorn looked over at my khakis and briefly took his right hand off the wheel to feel the material admiringly.

"I told him you are Canada ambassador in country," he said.

I could have throttled him right there as he sat at his steering wheel. Instead, I only sighed.

At length we came to a dirt road with a fork in it. One path led to a go-kart track, the other to the army camp. The camp, which had various obstacle courses and the like, seemed quite crowded and busy. There was a long queue of recruits in shiny new helmets waiting to climb to the top of a tall wooden tower and jump off the other side: part of their training to be parachutists. The uncle, whom Vorn told me was a colonel (he looked like a colonel all right), came out to greet us accompanied by two soldiers of other ranks, all of them wearing fatigues, but without any flashes or insignia. I was shown to a little wooden structure somewhat like a garden trellis. One stood under this facing an earthen track at the far end of which was a bull's-eye target.

"You can shoot at that," said the colonel, "or I can have a live chicken run across for you to shoot at."

I said the paper target would do just fine. He handed me an AK-47, showing me the safety and the selector switch.

Now over the years I've written "AK-47" any number of times in one book or another and in this or that piece

*A quiet street in the Old Quarter of colonial Hanoi in 1922.
Note the rickshaw passenger wearing a sola topi.*

France's hold on Indochina began with the acquisition of Saigon, occupied in 1862. These scenes show how thoroughly French the city looked six decades later — by which time Cambodia and Laos had also been assimilated.

149 — Souvenir des Ruines d'ANGKOR

In exploring the Mekong River as a possible trade route to China, the French "discovered" the holy city of Angkor in Cambodia, once the seat of Khmer civilization. In the 1870s, Europeans were transfixed by images of its abandoned temples.

When the Mekong proved less than perfect as a commercial high-way, the French pursued alternative routes in the neighbouring kingdoms of Annam, whose capital was Hué, and Tonkin, farther north, whose seat was Hanoi.

3111 — TONKIN
Conducteur de brouette
passant sous la porte de son village

Postcards of French Indochina, which flourished in the first quarter of the twentieth century, fall into a number of broad categories. Some show native inhabitants going about what seemed their quaint tasks, such as steering a wheelbarrow made of elephant tusks or rolling cigars and cigarettes.

3023. TONKIN — Hanoï
Petites Cigarières de la manufacture
de tabac

14 — Type de Notable Annamite

ANNAM — Vinh
Jeune femme

Also popular were portraits of local worthies — not as individuals, but as types, as with these two Annamite gentlemen. Attempts were also made to illustrate the various other social and economic classes, as with this somewhat prosperous Annamite woman (note her European clock) and this Tonkinese man.

Other postcards called attention to French Indochina's multi-cultural nature, as when they depicted an ethnic Chinese official in Tonkin, close to the border with China; a Malay in southern Cochinchina; or a group of Japanese dancers in Haiphong.

Type de Malais en Cochinchine

Collection Raquez — LAOS - Série A, n° 18
La plus gracieuse des Ballerines laotiennes

119. TONKIN — Hanoi - Servante Indigène

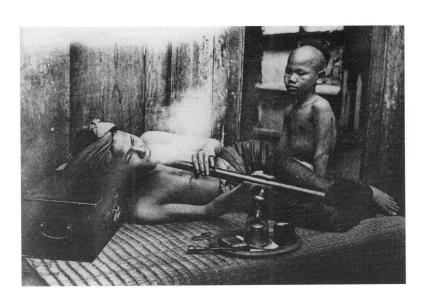

The urge to make postcards of French Indochina (and other tropical and subtropical colonies) into what the English called "French postcards" evidently could not be resisted, as with this popular image of a Lao dancer or the somewhat less prurient one of une tonkinoise. *For pedlars of the exotic, a posed scene in an "opium den" was also de rigueur.*

Whether as a royal seat or colonial capital, Phnom Penh never achieved the bustle of Saigon, the dignity of Hué, the charm of Hanoi — or even the peace and quiet of Vientiane. This view of its riverfront makes the point. Nonetheless, the city, like Cambodia as a whole, appealed to ethnologists and pornographers alike.

(121) CAMBODGE : Femmes Cambodgiennes au bain.

1686. CAMBODGE – PHOM-PENH
Samand, une des Premières Danseuses
de S. M. Sisowath

The French Republic naturally feared republicanism in its colonies, and so it kept the Indochinese monarchies in place. King Sisowath of Cambodia, who ruled from 1904 to 1927, the golden age of French ambition in the region, was expert at pretending to admire the French mission civilisatrice. *This portrait was taken in 1906, the year he made his first visit to Paris (he was sixty-six). His entourage for the trip included more than forty dancing girls from his court, such as the one shown here. Her name was Samand.*

A. T. III. - **Voyage aux Monuments Khmers**
SIEM-REAP. - La Pagode, face latérale

1784. Ex-Cambodge - ANGKOR-THOM
Les Tours à quatre visages

244. - RUINES D'ANGKOR. - Angkor Wat. - Petit Temple et Cour dallée du deuxième Etage.

*Then as now, Siem Reap was the gateway to Angkor Wat, one of
the world's most significant religious sites of antiquity.*

The Angkor complex is so vast that French scholars restored its main buildings in stages over more than a century, and such work continues even now. But Angkor's were hardly the only important Khmer temples in Southeast Asia, for the Khmer culture once covered much of modern Thailand and Laos, as well.

56 — PRAH KHAM. — L'un des édicules de l'entrée principale. Il présente ces admirables colonnes rondes, à peu près uniques parmi les monuments Khmers.

of reportage. I've made similarly cavalier use of the term "M-16" for the weapon developed by the United States in answer to the Soviet Union's Kalashnikov. Certainly I've often enough seen both weapons close up, as they have been shamelessly copycatted by other countries round the world. I've ever had them pointed at me. Please forgive my bad manners if I quote something I published a few years ago. Given the choice, I wrote:

> Some people will always choose the ripoff of the American technology while others inevitably would pick the AK-47 or one of its younger siblings, two of whose banana clips can be joined together with duct tape for twice its rival's load. Like PC and Mac users, or Coke and Pepsi drinkers, never the twain shall meet. One day there will be a war between people separated by nothing more than such preferences in the tools of war.

Until now, however, I had never actually been in a position to compare the two weapons. Now I fired a few thirty-round clips with each one, first single shots, then short bursts, and finally rock 'n' roll. The weapon designed for the Red Army by General Mikhail Kalashnikov when he was a sergeant is light, easy to handle, and mechanically simple. In a sense, it is the ballpoint pen of death; when it breaks, you throw it away and get another. The M-16 is more solidly constructed and more accurate. It's also heavier to carry and is said to be less reliable under certain conditions.

When I finished, the colonel was smiling at me. He offered me what he considered a special treat: the chance to fire an M-60 machine gun, one of those fed by a circular drum on top. It was a Chinese weapon of mature years, one I'd only ever seen in movies. It had a bipod, suggesting that it was to be fired from a prone position, but conditions at this makeshift range weren't set up for that, so I fired it while standing, first from the shoulder, then from the hip. I suppose I'm of average strength for a fellow of my age and skeletal frame, but I couldn't control the weapon very well, at least not on rapid fire.

I suspected that all the busy-ness at the camp, and maybe the reason Vorn was invited to bring me there for a look-see, had to do with the latest outbreak of ill will between Cambodia and Thailand about the eleventh-century temple complex the Khmers call Prasat Preah Vihear, but the Thais insist is named Khao Phra Vilharn. It is perched on a cliff 550 metres above the border between the two countries about 450 kilometres north of Phnom Penh. Centuries of Thai sovereignty over the spot ended with the 1907 treaty, but in 1959, the Thais grabbed it a second time, only to lose it again in 1962. Since then, emotions have boiled over frequently, as was the case at the time I'm describing, and the uneasy peace was being disturbed by exchanges of mortar and artillery fire.

In any event, I returned the ear plugs I had been lent, and was led away to a small display of landmines and booby traps. On the way back to Vorn's car, my ambassadorial boots were crunching over a thick stratum of discarded shell casings. Why they weren't being either recycled or sold for scrap, I couldn't imagine. I bent down and picked up a few for examination. They were Chinese.

— THE VICTORY GATE —

Vientiane, the capital of Laos, is a fading one-time French colonial outpost on a spot where a bend in the Mekong makes room for a large tear-shaped island directly opposite the centre-ville, which runs only far enough back from the riverbank to allow a few commercial streets. The new bridge to Thailand is only a short distance away. Thai-style wats and other temples, minor and major, are everywhere. Otherwise, barring the usual joint-venture hotels and such, the architecture is either Chinese-style shophouses, many of them quite elderly, or French buildings recalling the old days. The latter include the Presidential Palace, formerly the French governor's palace, and large French villas, expropriated at Independence, but left to ruin because no new use for them, or money to maintain them, could be found. They stand in overgrown lawns, their windows shuttered or punched out.

The most bizarre architectural remembrance of the French century is the Patuxai, or Victory Gate, a miniature copy of the Arc de Triomphe, sort of, but with enormous Buddhist spires on top. Such blending of French and Southeast Asian architectural styles became common in time, especially in Vietnam. This example stands at the terminus of the local equivalent of the Champs-Elysées. It is seven storeys high and contains stalls for the sale of knick-knacks. In other parts of the world, as well, the French enjoyed erecting monuments in the middle of traffic roundabouts. As I write these words, plans are afoot to rebuild the one that they put up in the middle of Rasheed Street in Baghdad, a once-grand boulevard that the American invasion turned into rubble. In Vientiane, neglect is more apparent than violence. This is not the case, however, in the more northerly part of the country.

In a sense, the Lao nation is more of a bald political construct than an organic expression of what's nonetheless, admittedly, an interesting and vibrant culture. For century after century, its people were under the control of either the Thais (their close cousins) or the imperial Chinese. The French didn't begin to insinuate themselves into the picture until after the Taiping Rebellion of 1845–65, instigated by a Chinese mystic named Hong Xiuquan who believed himself to be the brother of Jesus (not James, the one mentioned in the Bible — another one). He led China into the costliest civil war in world history, in which at least 20 million people were killed. After only eleven years in power, however, the rebels were driven from their capital, Nanjing, and decimated. The survivors, called Ho, dispersed into the mountainous no man's land in southern China where, in those days, the lines on the map separating China from northern hinterlands of modern Laos and Vietnam began to blur. There the Ho lived by plundering, kidnapping, murder, and extortion. They also fought one another. This was especially the case with two factions named for the colour of their battle flags. The French, who were nosing about, looking for a lucrative route to China, knew them as Les Pavillons Jaunes and Les Pavillons Noirs. The Black Flags were arguably the more frightening of the two. They also acted as mercenaries, retained by the Vietnamese emperor Tu Doc to fight the French who were in the process of taking over Tonkin and its capital, Hanoi. By the 1870s, the Ho, operating on their own account once again, had concentrated their villainy in modern Laos, including Luang Prabang and Vientiane.

Neighbouring cultures joined in the fighting, which was sometimes conducted from atop special war elephants. The one enemy common to all parties was disease. As a Lao historian puts it, the troops "died off like leaves" due to malaria. In the end, after a series of wars lasting into the mid-1880s and a talent for diplomatic deception and manipulation, the French were in full possession of Vietnam, consolidating their control by the usual steps, as the seized territory became a protectorate (as had been the case in Cambodia) and then a full colony. This still left Laos as a more complicated problem, for it was controlled by the Thais and coveted by the ever-dangerous British, who had colonized Burma, which was right next door and bordered India.

M and I began our assigned legwork. She called at such places as the Centre de la langue française, which she reported didn't seem especially well-used and was more or less indistinguishable from every little Alliance Française branch anywhere outside the Francophonie. She brought back the monthly programme. Language classes of course, a number of new books, and quite a few comics added to the library, the schedules of La Radio Nationale Lao (all the offerings in French) and Radio France Internationale (seven hours in French every day and one hour in Lao). Then she visited local elementary and secondary schools, where teachers told her that French was popular, but students said it wasn't.

For my part, I was oddly curious about the Victory Gate, but everyone I asked about its history had a different set of facts to offer. So I resorted to the official guidebook of the municipality published by Inter-Lao Tourisme. For a government publication it was jarringly frank in its tone: "At the North-Eastern extremity of the Lane Xang Avenue bears a structure resembling a big exquisite monument built in the form of Paris Arc de Triomphe [but which] hardly competes with the original's turbulent history and from a close distance, appears even less impressive, a monster of concrete." The booklet claims that the structure was built in 1962, but I've seen archival photos that show it surrounded by automobiles from the 1930s or 1940s. Maybe the booklet was correct and the city was once full of ageing cars. Old postcards also reveal that the avenue encircling it was well-paved, whereas now it is macadamized only with sticky red mud or a dusty crust of reddish dirt, depending on the season.

✳

George Fetherling

— CAPITAL SPLENDOURS —

M and I found a room in a Russian-built hotel with a view
of the river's south channel, with the Thai shoreline in the
distance. This was when the dry season was still playing itself
out, though the monsoon rains of late afternoon and early
evening brought temporary relief from the humidity while
softening the rugged clay soil for tilling. The water still being
low, the bank was planted in corn, which was about chest-
high despite not being well-hoed. We saw no commercial or
passenger traffic whatsoever on the river.

We strolled the length of the town, the river on our left,
the commercial strip — with the inevitable massage parlour,
mini-mart, and open-air Chinese restaurant — on the right.
More subtly so than the Patuxai, the buildings reveal the long
war between opposing traditions that never quite reconciled,
but only declared a truce. There are ornate French grilles on
windows that have never looked out on France of course,
but only on what their builders must have seen as the steady
encroachment of native ideas. M, who has spent time in West
Africa, said that the streetscape would fit perfectly into the
Côte d'Ivoire. But the faces, of course, are Asian, except for
the French faces, which are the same on either continent.

The hotel room had a strange piece of old wooden furniture about four feet high. The top third of it was a glass-fronted
box with a decorative handle for opening the glazed door. It
suggested a cabinet of curiosities or perhaps a place to exhibit
a wreath made from the hair of a deceased loved one, or some
other proof of lachrymose nineteenth-century sensibilities. In
fact, it turned out to be the primitive forerunner of the mini-
bar, an amenity supplemented by a daily bowl of fruit. This
one bit of charm aside, the room was true to its roots in the
period of a decade or so when design and construction projects
in Laos were undertaken routinely by experts from the Soviet

Union. By bombing Laos and Cambodia to keep them from following North Vietnam down the primrose path to communism, the Americans succeeded only in opening the way for government by the communist Pathet Lao forces, who enjoyed Moscow's support, and the regime of Pol Pot's Khmer Rouge, which carried genocide to new extremes.

When M and I were in Laos, the Soviet way of doing things was still being preserved in the system of vouchers, chits, and receipts employed at every opportunity, such as in what should be the simple matter of getting breakfast in the auditorium-like dining hall ("Performance from 0600 hrs," with riverfront roosters to ensure that we were there with time to spare). But then, to be fair, there were still everyday French cultural traits to observe. Yes, yes, baguettes — everybody always mentions the damn baguettes. More telling, because they indicate a style of administration rather than a quirk of cuisine, are the small red speed-limit signs, exactly like those in France. While I wandered about, M was trying to grapple with such matters as the carefully guarded minor distinctions between the programmes of, on the one hand, La Maison du Patrimoine and, on the other, those of L'ecole française Hoffet, which in this city of perhaps 160,000 people has 230 students enrolled in French-language classes. Both institutions are supposed to be operating at arm's length from the French embassy.

My desire was to go north to the Plain of Jars, which is said to be the most heavily bombed spot on Earth: not in terms of lives lost or the level of destruction, as in Hiroshima, Nagasaki, or Dresden, for it is a sparsely populated place, but rather in terms of the sheer tonnage of ordnance that the United States dropped there between 1964 and 1975 — on a country that was officially neutral, mind you. I was eager to see it, not merely because I remembered when it was very much in the news, but also because it is an important archaeological site, the most tangible reminder of a lost (and therefore mysterious) civilization, which French ethnographers and other scholars had studied for generations. What's more, it is a centre of one of the best-known ethnic minorities of Southeast Asia: the Hmong. Like their fellow mountain people, the Montagnards, the Hmong were fierce warriors who, while seeking autonomy, fought on the side of the French, first against the Japanese, then the Viet Minh, and later still on the side of the Americans against the North Vietnamese: an integral part of the CIA's famously "secret war." Their commander, Vang Pao (1929–2011), once a sergeant in the French army, later a nominal general in the Royal Lao Army, built and trained a guerrilla force of about forty thousand. William Colby, who headed the CIA in the mid-1970s, went so far as to call him "the biggest hero of the Vietnam War." When he died, in exile in the United States, the *Economist* labelled him, without complete accuracy, the "Montagnard Moses."

While still in Vientiane, waiting for our connection upcountry, M and I found a tiny so-called antique shop named Indochine, its name another proof that the term has become current again after shucking off decades of negative connotation, at least when divorced from France in particular. We had little doubt we'd find much detritus of French colonialism and thus benefit from a few minutes' tactile understanding of the old empire. No, the shop was chockablock with broken picture frames and purported silver flatware made of aluminium. And there was a bin full of cigarette lighters: replicas, shall we say, of the sort purchased by uncountable numbers of American soldiers and marines during the Vietnam War. They were universally called Zippos, after the Zippo Manufacturing Company of Bradford, Pennsylvania. During General Douglas MacArthur's occupation of Japan after Hiroshima and Nagasaki, *zippo* actually became the Japanese word for cigarette lighter, but the things were even more ubiquitous among the next generation of U.S. troops in Asia. Such lighters were available at every PX (post exchange) at $1.80 apiece. Ten million American military and naval personnel served in the former French Indochina during the American War. Many hundreds of thousands of them carried Zippos, which curbside artists would engrave for them with regimental crests or, more commonly, with protest slogans, to be kept in one's pocket, out of sight.

The wording on these ranged from bellicosity to bravado to well articulated fear. Examples include: GIVE ME YOUR HEARTS AND MINDS OR I WILL WRECK YOUR FUCKING HUT; STOLEN FROM A GOOK 5 11 67; 35 KILLS IF YOU'RE RECOVERING MY BODY FUCK YOU; and WHEN I DIE I'LL GO TO HEAVEN BECAUSE I'VE SPENT MY TIME IN HELL. Inevitably, there would be occasional outbreaks of complete nihilism as well, as with a Zippo that bears the following sentiment: FUCK HO CHI MINH/FUCK COMMUNISM/FUCK DEMOCRACY/FUCK UNCLE HO/FUCK UNCLE SAM/FUCK LBJ/FUCK V.C./FUCK SANTA CLAUSE [*sic*], FUCK YOU TOO. I take these representative texts from Sherry Buchanan, an independent scholar who studied important U.S. collections of the genuine article for her excellent book, *Vietnam Zippos: American Soldiers' Engravings and Stories 1965–1973*, which we could tell instantly the ones at Indochine were not, being made of the cheapest tin rather than steel and with the wording stencilled not engraved.

Browsing in the shop, M and I could see the two apparent co-proprietors in the back room watching television cartoons, one on the sofa, and the other on a straw mat on the floor. We had been there quite some time before the latter bestirred himself to welcome us. He was Vietnamese, by ethnicity if not by nationality. As about one-third of the people in Vientiane are Thais, this made him a second-tier minority. His eyes were mournful. He was in his twenties and had some English, whereas his much older partner (they're cousins, we discovered) spoke a little Russian.

And here lies the practical lesson we learned in Vientiane and took with us upcountry. Everyone in Laos seems to have a bit of a second language. With young people it's English, with their parents it's Russian, and with their grandparents it's French. "Listen," I said to M, who had never been in the region before. "When it looks like we're getting into trouble — and we may well — I'll grab the first kid I see and you find a grandmother quick." I pass along this travel tip. It worked every time.

— THE MELTING BUDDHA —

The nearest town to the Plain of Jars is Phonsavan in Xieng Khuang province. There are two ways to get there from Vientiane. You can take Highway 13 north for 350 kilometres or so before turning east on Highway 7. About midway between Vientiane and the turnoff is Vang Vieng. On first acquaintance the place pleases you with the way it's been kneaded in among the green-covered karst mountains. But it shocks you with its bigness as you've been passing through so many villages and hamlets along the way. They have names such Ban Phonmuang, Ban Senxum, and Ban Nammuang. *Ban* means village or simply dwelling. These are little brownish places, usually on some stream or river, with industrious but unhurried people (and animals). Laos has the lowest population density in Southeast Asia and one of the slowest metabolisms.

Vang Vieng is far enough south that it might be called the point at which the north begins. This is one factor that fills it with Western backpackers, including thrill-seekers hoping to be sold opium or lesser drugs. Or greater ones for that matter, such as, if reports are to be believed, powerful machine-rolled marijuana cigarettes soaked in liquefied heroin. These were one of the commodities that used to be available to American troops in Vietnam, presumably part of some secret North Vietnamese attempt to further demoralize them. Few activities are more dangerously illegal than drug-taking in Southeast Asia, but the practice continues all the same, despite constant pressure from the United States and some of its allies. (Other allies have begun to rethink the issue, given that 40 percent of the population of Laos are tribal people and that many of them are dependent on opium, which is a commodity in decline in the face of amphetamines — which the Lao call by the Thai name, *yaa baa* or "craziness drug.") Young Westerners, particularly those who push farther north and try not to stand out too starkly, have been known to lose all track of time. Doing so, they court a second kind of trouble, as long overstaying one's visa is another of the most felonious crimes under the Lao criminal code, which has existed only since 1990.

The alternative way of getting to Phonsavan from the capital is to fly in on a reconditioned Twin Otter. I passed on to M the warning not to be alarmed if the cabin suddenly filled with dark grey smoke, for that would be nothing more than the air conditioner catching fire again. The pilot followed the mountaintops, climbing and descending according to the height of each successive range. Every few minutes we would break out of cloud cover and see an ochre-coloured serpentine river twisted out of shape and getting smaller. At long intervals there would be a tiny village on the concave side of an elbow. The mountain ridges looked like sharp pieces of green glass.

From the sky, I could see how the old bomb craters were evenly spaced in straight lines, with the lines crossing and recrossing one another as sortie followed sortie. A funny thing about bomb craters. In Vietnam, the pace of development, especially since the late 1980s, has turned attention away from the destructiveness of the past. The fierce determination and practicality of the Vietnamese is an equally important factor in the process. You still see unreconstructed craters, but many others have been converted to round paddies or incorporated into irrigation systems or simply made into ponds for ducks or cattle and water buffalo. The Lao seem different. They're generally a more pessimistic and melancholy people. In Laos, what you see are barren yellow declivities in an otherwise lush landscape. People are routinely injured falling into them. So are animals, sometimes drowning.

The airport at Phonsavan consists of a short runway and two dirty one-storey structures. The smaller building appears to adhere loosely to the concept of the first-class lounge, for what are known throughout East Asia as "charming hostesses" were leaning out the open windows. The larger one, the terminal, was a single room with a big hand-lettered advertising sign: LAO AVIATION — ALL PASSENGERS ARE COVERED BY INSURANCE.

Nearing Phonsavan, one gets the first inkling that the Plain of Jars is not far off. Just west of there are fields with huge stone jars in the familiar shape, but left unfinished where they were being worked on. Their incomplete state suggests some sudden calamity, as do those *moai* on Easter Island that lie half carved in the quarry where they were being sculpted. One group of jars is close to what used to be Muang Sui, in its day a great centre of Buddhist worship that later became a staging area for U.S. bombing runs. After the American defeat, the newly reunited Vietnamese levelled the tainted place in the course of driving out the Royal Lao Army. Since then, a new town has been built on the spot and a great many Vietnamese have settled there.

There are numerous limestone caves — entire networks of them — throughout this area, and many ruined or looted wats and temples. The most dramatic ruin consists of a few still-upright pillars and an enormous centuries-old stone Buddha the side of whose face started to melt, like an ice cream cone, as a result of the great heat caused by the phosphorous bombs that also of course killed the community of monks. Close by is another shocking reminder of both the American War and the one that preceded it. It is the remnants, just a couple of metres high, of a large red-brick hospital, built by the French, bombed to smithereens by the Americans.

At first glance, and judging by Lao standards, Phonsavan is bustling right along, thanks to its role as the capital of Xieng Khuang province and investment by the nearby Vietnamese. Yet, paradoxically, it also seems little more than a sad and dilapidated Hmong market town, with rows of shophouses on either side of the partially paved roads. Bomb casings, particularly from the old 250-pounders (why none from the five-hundreds?), are propped up outside some of the small businesses or used in front gardens as fences or planters. There are still amputees walking the streets, though fewer than I feared. The government centre for the distribution of artificial limbs is located there.

Along the high street we saw few restaurants. This was a concern as M and I needed to find a meal and a place to stay before tracking down our local expert on Plain of Jars lore. Among M's sterling qualities, one of my favourites is the fact that she is such a game traveller. One can't beat a private school old-girl for laughing at discomfort and being indefatigable.

We found a low, dark eating-place, open to the street on two sides. In spots, the ceiling was only two metres high and one section of the floor was made of packed earth. The kitchen was an open stone hearth of the sort one sees in rural China. Sheets of sticky white plastic covered the plank tabletops and the seats were somewhat like milking stools. No one spoke French or English, and between us M and I didn't have a word of Lao or one complete sentence of Vietnamese. So we had only the vaguest notion of what we ate, except that we hoped it wasn't pork. For throughout the meal we heard the pitiful death-row squeals of a pig being dragged down the empty street to slaughter. At every step it dug its trotters into the dirt and tried to slip out of the rope round its neck. The two children taking it to be killed laughed at the creature's predicament, and so did our fellow diners — or all of them except a very old man whom the others had summoned to the restaurant to meet us, the two visiting big-noses from America or Europe. He shook our hands as firmly as he could, and we asked him to join us. He had a wrinkly upper lip and kind rheumy eyes. I would put his age at eighty-something. I imagine that M and I were having the same thought: "He's not mocking the poor pig simply because he himself is old and probably dying, but because he's lived through death round here his entire life."

The place we found to stay overnight was a kind of Alpine lodge, owned by a mature French woman to whom all the locals seemed to kowtow. M engaged her in conversation, but not for very long: the woman was simply not interested in talking to her guests. I thought perhaps she was one of the few who had chosen to stay on after Dien Bien Phu. I was reminded of the scene in the director's cut of *Apocalypse Now* about a French plantation family that had done just that (a scene that spoiled the movie's pace, showing once again why certain scenes are deleted for narrative reasons).

Outside the woman's front door was a 250-pound bomb, a dud, its nose stuck in the ground, around which a tree had been growing for all these years. Had it exploded on impact as it was supposed to, the chalet and its residents would have perished in an instant.

— THE TARGET ZONE —

Khan, our local expert, was born and reared in Luang Prabang, the old royal capital on the winding Mekong, the place where we would be heading in a couple of days. When he was a boy, his father wished him to learn French. Apparently the father was older than the norm when Khan was born in 1976 and so was harking back to his own youth when French was a requirement for an ambitious young Lao who wished to get ahead in the established order. Khan studied for only a couple of months. "I was not liked by French," he remembered. "Everything was *le*, *la*, *les* ..." He finished the sentence with a Gallic shrug, brushed hair from his eyes, and took a drag on his cigarette, readjusting the minuscule waist of his grey pleated trousers. His family then countered that he take up Russian, for Russian was still somewhat in fashion, though he found that language, too, to be uncongenial. But he knew he had a knack for English, which is to say a knack for making money. He knew what he was taking us to see, but I wondered how much he knew about why foreigners, particularly ones of a certain age, were interested in going there.

Much later, back home in Canada, I came upon the following item in the *Globe and Mail*, paraphrasing a news story that had appeared in the paper fifty years earlier, on August 24, 1959: "The *Globe and Mail* reported that pro-communist Pathet Lao insurgents attacked and infiltrated parts of Vientiane province, within 50 miles of the Laotian administrative capital city of Vientiane. Although unconfirmed by Laotian defence officials, Western military sources said the insurgents attacked two army posts within a 70-mile radius." And thereby, at least by suggestion, hangs the entire tale.

Assimilating (a polite term) a place as wild as Laos wasn't an easy task for the French or an inexpensive one. It was in 1907 — the year of so many of the postcards in this book, long after Cambodia and the parts that now make up Vietnam were somewhat stable and at least temporarily safe — that the French got control of all the Lao land on the east side of the Mekong, facing Siam. The Japanese kicked them out during the Second World War, but they returned in 1945 in a massive airborne operation and re-declared the Protectorate. When the local population did not respond by lining the streets waving Tricolours on little sticks, the French granted them status as an independent associated state and then, in a surprisingly short time, full sovereignty. But this resulted in a coalition government that the United States brought down, only to be left with the fear that the Pathet Lao communists would win a majority in the election to be held in 1960 — which, therefore, the CIA shamelessly rigged. In that simpler time and smaller world, the CIA station in Vientiane was one of the agency's largest, though it had only three hundred agents (the same number as Miami's). They were under the command of Lawrence R. Devlin, who had just arrived there from Congo where as chief of station he was concerned — innocently so, he professed — in the assassination of Patrice Lumumba, the deposed prime minister.

Of course this was several years after France lost its hold on Indochina as a result of the battle of Dien Bien Phu. The United States had now taken upon itself the ridiculous responsibility for interfering in Southeast Asian affairs. Assuming office in 1961, the new chief executive, John F. Kennedy, made a display of saying that he would invade Laos if necessary. At that point, a curious moment in history seemed to come about. Would the United States attack Vietnam, where communists held power in the north, or Laos, where they were merely, in the American view, waiting in the wings? I have no doubt that Vegas bookmakers were giving odds. In his autobiography, Peter C. Newman, the famous Canadian journalist, remembers being asked to choose between reporting from Vietnam or reporting from Laos, as his editor in Toronto wouldn't pay for both. Newman made the wrong choice: Laos. Arriving there, he was surprised to discover that Laos, which is landlocked, had a Royal Laotian Navy. A thirty-foot gunboat launched in 1904 was the only fully operational warship. A number of the others, made of rotting wood, were hauled up on the banks of the Mekong for use as chicken coops.

That Kennedy decided to terrorize Vietnam instead (though the great build-up took place under his successors) enraged the military and intelligence establishment who feared that he would wimp out on both alternatives. There is a memorable scene in the Oliver Stone film *JFK* that depicts a meeting of such hawks. One of them says angrily, "He fucked us in Laos, and now he's going to fuck us in god-damn Vietnam!" But it was in 1964, the year after Kennedy's assassination, when the U.S. bombings began. Before they were over, 2 million tons of explosives had been dropped on a small area that the U.S. believed was the marshalling yard of the amorphous Ho Chi Minh trail, which the communists used to help resupply their troops in the field. The weight of the bombs dropped on Laos and Cambodia by the U.S. was greater than that of all those dropped on Europe during the entire Second World War, according even to Robert S. McNamara, the American defense secretary in the Kennedy and Johnson administrations.

— AMONG THE HMONG —

I was full of questions about the Hmong that I hoped Khan could answer, but he couldn't. He turned out to be less than expert in his Local Knowledge. For example, within sight of the largest collection of jars is a ruined and abandoned temple. It is a tower made of blocks of laterite, wide at the base, but redented as it rises toward the pointed crown, with each step almost completely covered by who knows how many generations of unchecked plant growth. It certainly looks like the simplest type of Khmer chapel, but in what's now Laos, the Khmer culture didn't penetrate farther north than Vientiane. Was this, rather, what's known as a *prang* in Thailand, where Khmer ruins are conspicuous in many regions, and, what's more, left their design influence on Thai Buddhism? Khan seemed to lack even the broadest historical understanding of who was where and when. Maybe the lesson to be gleaned from his deficiencies as a comprador is an awareness that today's national borders are political, not cultural; that belief systems were passed back and forth, mutating as they did so; and that the French, for better or for worse — and, in some ways, obviously both — were a unifying and codifying cultural force and not merely money-grubbing power-grabbers, though, like all the European colonial powers, they certainly were that, as well.

Khan may have been unable to impart much knowledge even about the abundant Hmong, but he did lead us into their front garden, so to speak. The Hmong are one of the important ethnic minorities of Laos and Thailand. They dislike being called mercenaries, but using a softer term is as much a matter of tact as of accuracy. During the eight years when the U.S. waged a secret war in Laos, using Hmong tribesmen, sometimes in battalion-sized units, to fight the Pathet Lao, the most intense violence took place where we were going now.

We drove to the summit of one of the nearby hills. This was as far as we could travel in Khan's vehicle as beyond that the road had become a mere muddy rut. We then continued on foot, over meadows with stunted conifers, and, way off in the background, the mountains of Vietnam (Dien Bien Phu is about 125 kilometres away). This description makes it sound pleasant enough, and viewed in broad perspective at the right time of the year it is indeed scenic. But the spot formerly called la Plaine des Jarres must be one of Southeast Asia's spookiest places, a large, flat region, surrounded by mountains as high as three thousand metres and never completely free of disfiguring mist. The stone jars that litter the site (it's a marvel that so many survived the bombing, even in pieces) are thought to have been made two thousand years ago, around the time the Hmong first migrated southward from Mongolia, a place of origin that can still be read in their faces. But the ancestors of the Hmong did not produce these jars. In fact, specialists tell us, they bear no discernible trace of the Tibetan, Chinese, Khmer, Indian, Viet, or Cham cultures, though virtually all of these people fought battles on the spot over the centuries.

Each jar is carved from a single rock or boulder, most of them limestone, but some are granite. The jars vary in size according to the size of the raw material. At the biggest of the several clusters scattered over the meadows, the largest jar is 2.5 metres high and quite wide (I could have stood up in it), but most are a great deal smaller. Some have stone covers.

Many theories have been advanced about their use. Some speculate that they were for collecting water during the dry season; others argue that they were for storing rice for use during times of famine, or even for fermenting it. Still others hold that they were intended for votive or funereal purposes. An anthropologist in the 1930s claimed to have found human bones in some of the jars, but this evidence and other artifacts have been lost. French photographs from the early twentieth century show figurative carvings on at least a couple of jars, but these features, too, were destroyed long ago. Now there's only one lichen-covered jar that is said to have a sort of petro-glyph of a human figure. Seeing the image, however, requires a great deal of faith and imagination. In any case, most of the field work and scholarly writing on the subject, until recent times especially, had been done by the French, who had patiently labelled, documented and studied each specimen. A disproportionate amount of the labour was the initiative of the admirable Ecole Française D'Extrême-Orient (representing the positive side of French colonialism). Madeleine Colani, a famous archaeologist, was one of the great figures in the field. Her book *Megalithes du Haut Laos*, published in 1935, is the seminal work, and I deeply regret not having bought the mildewed copy I once found in a box of junk under a rickety table at a hole-in-the-wall second-hand bookshop in Saigon (where I also spotted copies of the *Associated Press Year Book* and related items no doubt left behind hurriedly during the dramatic climax of the American War).

Odd to say, but the main Plain of Jars site smells like England. Close up, it feels and looks somewhat like England, too. There's flint underfoot. Rounded green hills recall the Cotswolds. But when you look further and more closely, you see strange contradictions. The lookalike Cotswolds are backed up by a lookalike Swiss Alpine slopes and the whole scene is plopped down in the middle of the mountain rain-forest that covers much of Southeast Asia. There's a weird combination of flora: a few cacti, and trees that are close cousins of the Ponderosa pine, but also gum trees of the sort found in tropical Australia. The area seems pieced together using leftover bits from other climatic zones.

Such is the landscape today. Speculating about the land-scape and climate two millennia ago is of course difficult at best and possibly foolhardy. At this particular location there has been relatively little development; and while the climatic cycle may have changed, the basic fact of alternating wet and dry seasons probably has not. As there is no river or other year-round source of water close by, it may well be that the jars, or some of them, were used to store up water during the monsoon. The design of the surviving lids, which have circular runnels for channelling rainwater, points to this. So does the fact that even today many Lao in this part of the country have primitive hand-dug wells. The very shape of the vessels, with walls of a uniform thickness and exterior sides straight rather than curved, is ideal for keeping evaporation to a minimum. My feeling, one supported by absolutely no one else as far as I know, is that all the labour involved in making such containers points to a highly valuable crop, probably one requiring all the more help during the dry season because it's one that matures only once a year. And I think we can guess what it might have been. When I visited the Plain of Jars, the local Hmong had finished the annual harvest of opium poppies only ninety days earlier, before the rains began.

The time before the rains was not always an easy abstraction to keep in mind when M and I were there, given the intensity of the sporadic downpours and their cumulative effect on the roads. On our way back from the site, we had to take shelter in a tall, narrow cave with three chimneys at the top that permitted narrow shafts of light to reach the floor, where several small Buddhist shrines had been erected. A nearby resident told us that during the American War, local people fled to this cave and one other whenever bombing raids began. Then the caves were themselves bombed. The number of people killed is a matter of dispute, to judge from the fact that everyone I asked had a different figure. But the locals swear that as late as the 1980s, a decade and a half after the incident, visitors still smelled the faint odour of dead bodies inside the cave.

Red mud, the sort familiar to readers of the memoirs that war has produced, kept us from driving to the second jars site, about twelve kilometres distant. But we got as close we could, and then hiked the rest of the way. So much heavy mud stuck to our shoes that I felt like an old-time deep-sea diver walking the ocean floor in leaden boots. My trousers were filthy, too. I considered rolling them up to the knee but had been told this was an open invitation to leeches. The mess would soon be worse: cross dark clouds seemed to be holding a council overhead.

This second site is higher up, smaller and more compact than the first, but no better preserved. Though a great many lie in pieces, the jars are found around the rims of craters. And yet on the same site I saw something that lifted my spirits. I found one ugly crater with a mature tree growing in it. Then I saw another. More than thirty years have passed and time has pushed on. At some level a new generation has forgotten the horror. Nature, it seems, is forgetting, too.

As for the Hmong, 3 million of them live in China and more than half a million in Vietnam. The lesser numbers elsewhere in Southeast Asia, including Burma, have never been counted accurately. All Hmong share a common language, but they are distinguished from one another by the dominant colours on their jackets and headdresses. Blue Hmong and White Hmong are numerous in Vietnam, for example. Those in Laos and Thailand are known as Green Hmong and can be divided further by their palette, and more importantly, by their politics.

Vietnam's Hmong sided with the communists in the early 1960s, while those in Laos were recruited by the CIA. All had fearsome reputations as combatants. The anti-communist ones were officially paid by the rightist Lao government, but the money came from the United States, which also armed and trained them. When the military effort failed, thousands of Hmong fighters, rightly fearing for their lives, fled to the United States. As a result, the largest Hmong population outside Asia, about fifty-eight thousand people, is in Fresno, California, with several smaller enclaves elsewhere in the state. Minneapolis, of all places, has the highest concentration outside the west coast. In recent years, more and more have been allowed to immigrate to the United States.

The Hmong in Laos — the ones who take such exception to being lumped in with their relatives and friends who worked for the CIA — are hill people, like nearly all Asian Hmong, and generally keep to elevations above eight hundred metres — far above, if they can. They live by growing maize and sometimes opium by slash-and-burn methods, and by hunting. Every year on the Plain of Jars, Hmong are injured, maimed, or killed by UXO — unexploded ordnance — once dropped from American B-52s. The most common and deadliest of these leftovers are the fist-sized sachets of explosive once used in cluster bombs. Hmong hunters seek them out for the gunpowder they contain. Foreigners visiting the area are advised to stick closely to the narrow footpaths and hire a Hmong to lead the way, and then follow in the prints of his or her flip-flops.

— THE VIEW FROM PHU SI —

Everyone enjoys going to Luang Prabang, which is a UNESCO World Heritage site, and justifiably so. It is perhaps the best-preserved fully functioning ancient city in Southeast Asia. It sits, with a generalized air of gentle timelessness, perched along an especially beautiful stretch of the Mekong. *Luang* translates as *Royal*, as this small city (the population has merely doubled in the past century and a half) was the first seat of the original Lao Kingdom, the Lan Xang. That was in 1357. When the administrative functions were moved downstream to Vientiane in 1545, it became a sort of city-state while remaining part of the kingdom. But it became a kingdom in its own right in 1707 when the Lan Xang splintered into three parts. It held that position, with a couple of embarrassing interregna, until the Pathet Lao formed the present republic in 1975.

Northern Laos was one of the last pieces the French needed to complete their Indochina jigsaw puzzle. They hovered nearby as the puny kingdom was raided and robbed by the Burmese, the Siamese, and the Vietnamese. Then in

1887, the Pavillons Noirs came pouring down the Nam Pa, which flows into the Mekong from the east a few kilometres north of the city. The attack was so devastating that the king had to bargain with France for permanent protection. The French allowed the monarchy to remain, intact and essentially powerless, inside the palace (now a museum).

One of the first French initiatives in Luang Prabang was to put up a building called the Commissariat. In a city characterized by smallish two-storey hybrids (French brick at street level, Lao wood construction up above — most dating from the Postcard Age, with a few from the 1950s), this was a big structure indeed. These days it has been rebuilt beyond recognition and is the forty-room Phousi Hotel, where M and I were staying. It is just down the road from the Hmong market on Thanon Setthathilat, the long street distinguished by the sorts of businesses that Westerners favour: a foreign-language bookshop, a highly calorific bakery, an Internet café, and so on. There can be few such high streets in Southeast Asia less severely marred by tackiness and hucksterism.

Craft items are the main draw in the stalls at the Hmong market, particularly clothing and accessories. There are trousers and square tops made of hemp cloth, perpetuating traditional motifs in startlingly bright colours along with black. The batik work is of high quality, but then dyeing is a Hmong art form, as with indigo skirts (ones actually made by boiling the indigo plant) that are then decorated with red. All girls are taught needlework (*paj ntaub*, literally "flower cloth") from an early age. By puberty they have already amassed the wardrobe that is to carry them along in married life. The Hmong are wild about elaborate hats and wide-strapped shoulder bags with mythological designs, both of which look rather Tibetan in character to Western eyes. They are also avid fans of jewellery, including finely made necklaces and bracelets fashioned from ropes of silver rings.

There were some staple foods for sale at the Hmong market, as well: rice of course, maize, cane, peanuts, green beans, squash, cucumbers, and an edible root called manioc. But the main farmers' market is elsewhere and operates in the early mornings. It is an orderly assemblage of people buying what they need for the evening table. By contrast, the night market, down by the waterfront, is more Chinese in character, in that it's jam-packed with sharp-elbowed bargain hunters straining their eyes under the strings of electric lights to determine, by feel and by smell, the best possible example of each species of fish while, at the same time, arguing or gossiping with everyone else in the crowd.

The city always has been and continues to be the spiritual centre of the country. Most of it sits on a thumb-shaped peninsula, in the middle of which is a single, large hill — in the circumstances, one might almost say a miniature mountain — called Phu Si. This is home to four of Luang Prabang's thirty-three surviving temples, some of them five hundred years old. They vary considerably in their architecture. One can only imagine what the city was like before the French takeover, when there were sixty-six temples.

One climbs Phu Si by a long series of steep steps on the west side. For some, this walk is related to religious observance of course; for others it is a matter of sightseeing. Going up to the summit was one of the first things we did on arriving, for we wanted to take in the 360-degree view before the light faded. At the peak, where in another culture with a different history one might expect to find some sort of statue or memorial, there are instead the rusting remains of a Russian anti-aircraft emplacement. On the north side, one looks out over the Nam Kha far below, a wide smear of brownish water winding its way along toward its union with the Mekong. Running more or less parallel to it was the then still notorious Highway 1, which had recently experienced a resurgence of bandit activity. It was as though the ghosts of the Pavillons Noirs had not been put to rest, or were somehow being honoured.

⚜ ✳ ⚜

— BUDDHAS AND BATS BY THE THOUSANDS —

M and I were up not much past dawn, evidently the same as everyone else, and we went down to the river, where the homes, and the people as well, are visibly poorer than those just a few steep steps away. A storm overnight had shredded the plastic sheets used as awnings; strips of the stuff were tangled round the unpainted balustrades on back galleries of the buildings that overlook the river. Palm fronds were lying everywhere; discarded water bottles rolled back and forth, up and down Thanon Khem Khong. We wanted to go upriver about twenty-five kilometres to the mouth of the Nam Ou, the place where the warlords had come in such force, though for most visitors the purpose of such a trip is to marvel at the Buddha-filled Pak Ou caves (which we would also do).

We suffered only minor confusion figuring out where to catch a longtail boat at the so-called Mail Boat Pier, which is the seat of north-south river traffic, but not of the ferries that trundle back and forth. The boat we boarded was a family operation, steered by the father while the mother, who was also the deckhand, cooked for the family, and one of the children did his schoolwork near the bow. It rode so low in the water that without leaving my seat or even leaning over, I could almost have plunged my hand in the Mekong. The vessel had a homemade appearance yet reminded me of a European railway carriage, with square windows along both sides, with strips of cotton used to tie back the curtains.

There are hamlets on both the east and west banks. We stopped to take a look at one of the best known of these villages, Ban Xang Hai — best known because it is a village of jar makers (that is what the name means). Modern commerce being what it is, big brown clay jars are purchased from an outside source and used to hold the rough Lao rice wine called *lào-lào*. Archaeologists have found that the site was inhabited two thousand years ago. When we put in there, it first seemed to be inhabited no longer, as the rain had returned with enough force to drive indoors the handful of residents who weren't working somewhere else that day. We climbed up the slippery red mud hill, falling several times. The houses were in a ragged row up a steep, winding path, like a lonely scribble in the jungle. They were built on pylons about 1.5 metres high, so as to limit damage during floods and provide storage for the inventory of jars and shelter for the animals the rest of the time. Hens with black spots were puttering about while the chicks sat protected under reed-woven domes that looked like big overturned laundry baskets. One building stood out from the others for being much taller and being open to the elements on all four sides. This was the school. I saw no books or blackboards there, but only a haunting poster illustrating fifteen different varieties of landmines and grenades. Someone confirmed that the text in Lao was a warning to young ones not to touch or play with such things when found. Later, I saw the identical poster, but with Khmer writing, in Phnom Penh. It now hangs in my flat, prompting a cautionary tale that always needs retelling.

In the dry season, which this most definitely was not, the water is so low that boats have to leave from an alternative jetty in Luang Prabang where the water is deeper. At such times, sandbars are exposed to view, and many Lao paddle over to the ones near where the Nam Ou empties into the Mekong and pan for gold — how successfully, I have no idea. We saw only fishers instead, casting their nets or — the perpetual chore of fishers — mending them. Artifacts found above the Nam Ou near the confluence date back eight thousand years. There is a Hmong village high up on the north bank, but it isn't visible, not that time of year, at least, from the stairs on the opposite shore of the Mekong. These are the steps that lead to the lower-most of the enormous and enormously sacred limestone caves, famous for containing literally thousands of Buddha figures, especially (but not only) the standing one associated with Luang Prabang. The upper cave is slightly more difficult to access, has fewer statues and figurines, is also darker, and is inhabited by an uncountable number of bats.

Back in Luang Prabang the next day, M and I set out on our self-assigned tasks. Poking about one of the back lanes, I discovered a discarded metal sign that obviously had once hung on a government building. It was perhaps 1.5 metres in height and two in width, and shaped like royal crown; it was emblazoned with a big yellow hammer and sickle. Many dwellings and temples were freshly whitewashed, the streets were clean and quiet. I stood in the shade of lotus trees and smelled the bougainvillea blossoms. Occasionally I would see a bright multicoloured jumbo, a form of public transport larger than a *tuk-tuk*, but smaller than one of the buses (which are small in any case). Bicycles are by far the most common form of vehicular traffic, though rentals are not allowed and so only residents ride them (often steering with one hand while deftly manipulating an umbrella with the other). The town was busy and full of tourists, but I experienced nothing to jar the senses until a group of monks came up the street in close order, carrying their begging bowls. A Western woman with two cameras round her neck suddenly appeared out of the shadows to photograph them. They paid no attention, but she moved ever closer to them as her cameras clicked and clicked. I could see that she was about to touch the sleeve of one of them, presumably to ask if he would stop for a moment and pose for her. He evaded her, neatly, quietly, without expression, and without adjusting his step. I am normally a strong proponent of minding my own business, but in this case I took the woman aside and explained, with tact and patience, I thought, that the man would have had to perform a kind of purification ritual if she had touched him. She reacted badly to the news. Finally she said, "I'm going to see the abbot about this and give him a piece of my mind."

M, meanwhile, was busily researching French education to determine how it did or did not differ from that in Vientiane. She began with the *Golden Page Lao Business Directory*, which is the telephone book for the entire country, printed in Lao and English, but not French (a bad sign). It is devoted almost exclusively to businesses and in any case doesn't always make clear, not to foreign eyes, anyway, which entries refer to which towns and cities. By quietly muttering her frustration, however, she attracted the attention of the Phousi Hotel's desk clerk, who proved to speak French at what she called a "tourist-industry level." He told her that French-language classes are held at the school located behind the hotel. She went there and found a poster indicating that *classes bilingues*, parts of the Maison du Patrimoine programme, are held at 1600 hours.

She returned at the specified hour and waited and waited until students began arriving for some other class entirely. "Two teenage girls on motorbikes," she told me later, over dinner at a strange restaurant, open-air and bare-bones, down on the riverfront near the jetty. "Once they parked, they stopped to read something written in Lao on a big signboard. So I picked my way through the mud puddles and began a conversation with them in French. They giggled. One of them pulled out her textbook for the evening. Its title was *Lao-English Conversation Book*, so I thought I must be in the wrong place or in the right place at the wrong time." But she is not one to give up, and so whipped out her all-purpose *Southeast Asian Phrase Book* and the three of them tried to conduct a conversation using any Lao or English phrases that seemed to fit.

"There was a lot of laughing," she told me. "I found out that they were fifteen years old. They asked my name and where I was from and what I did for a living. They told me their names, but I couldn't record them because I found them hard to understand and was too busy looking things up. They told me they'd been taking English classes for three months.

"Soon five of their friends arrived and joined the conversation, and I was surrounded by about thirty teenage girls and twenty motorbikes. A few boys joined us. Finally one of the bolder girls gestured to me and said, 'Come, meet teacher.' He was in his classroom opening the doors and windows to let in some air. He was a young Lao who had been learning and teaching English for two years, and kept apologizing that his English wasn't better. He explained that the daytime school was out now but that young people are so eager to learn English that they show up at evening classes. All of these ones were students from a high school nearby.

"I naturally asked him about French class. 'Finished,' he said. 'Teacher gone home — home to France.' I first thought this meant that the classes weren't being offered any longer, but later found out that evening classes in French are only held during the regular school year.

"He invited me to be interviewed by the class. Everyone was so helpful, I could hardly refuse. So there I was standing at the head of the class, wearing my Jim Thompson silk T-shirt with the elephant on it, and they asked me questions. I chose 'build websites' as my answer to 'What do you do?' They understood what websites are (with help from the teacher, who wrote the English on the board). But when I asked them if they used email or went on the Internet — again, the teacher wrote the words on the board — no one put up a hand. He explained that they knew about these things, but didn't use them themselves." Mind you, this was a few years ago now; I'm certain the situation has changed greatly.

M continued: "I asked them their favourite singers or TV programmes, but they didn't have enough English to describe these to me. So after another ten minutes of conversation that, unfortunately, seemed not to be leading anywhere, I thanked the teacher for introducing me to his students and said I'd better let him get on with his class."

At this point our waiter arrived, carrying some sort of vegetarian plate for me and river eels for M, who is of course braver than I am.

"It turned out that my elephant shirt helped me make a good impression," said M. "It's a very positive image. Anyway, I found it satisfying to be on display myself for once as opposed to what we've been doing: floating by the local people and peering into *their* intimate lives whenever possible."

— THE YOUNG OXONIAN —

At Hong's Coffee Shop, I fell into conversation with a thin young woman who was exploring Laos, and quite thoroughly, before returning to her studies at Oxford. She was travelling light, on the back of her male friend's motorbike. We talked about the oddly beautiful riverboats that carry both cargo and passengers up and down the river. They're long wooden vessels, barge-like, but with high, square sterns like junks, and are painted Mediterranean blue with red trim.

"I wonder how long it would take to go down to Vientiane on one of them."

I said I didn't know, but obviously the downward trip would be much faster than the reverse, particularly now, in the wet season. (Later I checked. The passage from the Mail Boat

Pier in Luang Prabang to the Kao Liaw Pier in Vientiane is 430 kilometres and usually takes three days.)

"The thing that puts me off the idea," she said, "is that part at the back." She explained that she was referring to the outhouse suspended over the stern. "Mind you, we stayed in a hostel where everybody showered together and the partitions only came up to here." She indicated a spot midway between breasts and stomach. Anyway, she went on, she would be sticking to the motorbike for this trip. Maybe next time, if there ever were to be a next time.

We talked about Xieng Khuang Province and the Plain of Jars, and she told me about her problem. The motorbike had broken down and she and her partner had to locate a mechanic. "Well, not a mechanic actually. He was more of a tinker. He did things like take four old broken electric fans and, using bits from three of them, made one that worked. He had to rebuild our bike, but of course didn't have the right parts, so he used, what do you call it? An elbow? Yes, an elbow on the exhaust pipe. This is the result."

She twisted round in her chair and rolled up the right trouser leg. The newly improvised exhaust system was now sending the exhaust toward her, not away from her, and she had a circular burn on her calf the size of a doll's head. "You see, I was wearing shorts most of the time, and the bloody machine was roasting my flesh." It was clear that the fearsome-looking burn hadn't begun to heal. I urged her to go to a Chinese-run clinic I'd spotted the previous day. She shrugged and said that she and her boyfriend had to be off. They were heading straight up Highway 1. I warned her, calmly, I hoped, about its dangerous reputation. I also mentioned the added danger that the government's assurances that the problem had been eliminated might not be completely reliable, though I had no knowledge of the situation personally and was simply urging caution.

She laughed. "I have to keep moving, you see. It's an impulse hunger."

I wished her a safe trip and a happy life. I thought of her again when I got back to Canada and found the following news story from Hua Phan Province, immediately east of Luang Prabang, near the Vietnam border:

> The U.S. State Department has warned Americans of new security threats in Laos after five people were killed in an ambush on a bus in the latest of a series of deadly attacks in the country this year. Lao officials said a bus was ambushed on the road between Xam Neua and Vieng Xai, former headquarters of the communist Pathet Lao rebels during the Vietnam War. Radio Free Asia's Lao service said the ambush was carried out by ethnic minority people angry with the communist regime.

⇥ ✳ ⇤

— A ROOFTOP TOAST —

I had a special mission, a private one, not connected to the question of French culture, when I arrived in Saigon. I wanted to honour a late friend of mine. When he died in 1997, I wrote in the *Globe and Mail*: "The fact that he was rich was the least interesting thing about Charles Taylor." Charles was the son of E.P. Taylor, perhaps the most famous, feared, despised, envied, and editorially cartooned Canadian businessman of the 1950s. To say the least, Charles went off in a direction different from his father's, becoming, to quote myself again, an "author, foreign correspondent, Sinologist, bon vivant [and] horse breeder." When he died, after the most appalling nine-year struggle with cancer, he was sixty-two and had published five books. One of them, *Radical Tories: The Conservative Tradition in Canada*, which appeared in 1982 (and reissued in 2006), was later named by the readers of the *Literary Review of Canada* as one of the hundred most important Canadian books of all time.

It's a book as odd as it is delightful. As he confesses to the reader, Charles had paid scant attention to Canadian politics as a young man, because he was busy with international affairs. He put the *Globe*'s Beijing bureau on a permanent footing and covered wars, elections, and other excitements in fifty countries, armed with no other language than English, quick wits, a lively intelligence, and an attractive personality (which I seem to have described as "enormous well-scrubbed charm and bonhomie"). He had been everywhere and had known everyone. He once told me offhandedly, without the slightest affectation, that he couldn't remember whether he'd met the queen or not.

For Charles, as for so many people at the time, the American War changed everything. In his case, it had the effect of turning his attention homeward. In the common view, the war was waged by America's blinkered technocrats and by MBAs who believed they had only a management problem they thought they could solve by throwing money at it; the moral dimension eluded them. Charles gradually withdrew from journalism to write seriously about the war and later, by extension, about moral (not moralistic) conservatism, whose ideas derived from Edmund Burke, "who saw the state as a partnership not just among the living, but among those who are living, those who are dead, and those who are yet to be born." He became much influenced by Red Tory intellectuals such as the poet Dennis Lee (and non-intellectuals, too), the people associated with the deification of George Grant and the snootily superior brand of Canadian nationalism derived partly, and somewhat paradoxically, from the ideas of the German philosopher Martin Heidegger, the one-time member of the Nazi Party who in Western academic life today is considered one of the three or four most influential thinkers of the twentieth century.

I simplify outrageously, of course. The point is that Charles began to seek out some version of Canadian conservatism that he could feel comfortable with. *Radical Tories* and his closely related book *Six Journeys: A Canadian Pattern* (1977) were the result. Both are widely beloved for the grace and good humour of their prose.

Radical Tories is a series of linked essays — appreciations really — of Donald Creighton, W.L. Morton, Al Purdy, Eugene Forsey, Robert Stanfield and David Crombie. Note that only Creighton was a proudly bigoted person, with his lifelong aversion to the Québécois. And note that most of them are historians, as was, in his heart, Al Purdy, whose work probably has never had a finer, more understanding or more stylish piece written about it. Charles called him "a folk tory," using the lower-case *T* to make clear that he's not talking here about the old Progressive Conservative Party, but rather a turn of mind.

What distinguishes *Radical Tories* is first of all its felicitous writing (for example, John Kenneth Galbraith, at six-foot-eight, "moves with the awkward lope of a man in constant apprehension of upsetting the furniture"). It grudgingly has some fine things to say about individual members of the Liberal Party and occasionally takes individual Conservatives to task. In the end, it's not a book about partisan politics in the least. Charles was rather like Dalton Camp (who was rather like Benjamin Disraeli): a Conservative simply because he hated the Liberals for their power. He was either a small-*c* liberal or a small-*l* conservative, I'm not sure which, and it doesn't matter; and most of the figures he singles out for praise as Red Tories might just as easily be revered as Blue Grits.

Charles's intent needs no refreshing because it is timeless, despite the outdatedness of his examples. What seems to me to be his key statement falls near the middle of the book. He writes: "For most of this century, Canada has seen the triumph of the liberal levellers, secular Calvinists who despise anyone or anything which has claims to quality and finer feeling. Jealous and spiteful, they would cut everyone and everything down to their own level of insipid mediocrity. To survive in such a grudging milieu, those who strive for excellence often feel the need to mask their real intentions. Learned early, the impulse soon becomes instinctive."

Why do I go into all this now? Because I wished to honour his memory somehow now that I was in Saigon. He was fourteen years my senior, and was always trying to teach me lessons about journalism (a hopeless task, I fear). For example, he would tell me about how in Washington he would eschew the flashy presidential press conferences to spend days in a stuffy room where a subcommittee of a subcommittee of Congress was droning on about two sentences in a tariff bill that directly affected two hundred Canadian jobs. Or about how, when covering the war in Saigon, he refused to stay with all the other correspondents at the Continental or Caravelle hotels. Instead, he lived at the Rex, where the rooftop bar was actually owned and run by the propaganda arm of the American state department. At the Rex, you see, he got to talk with mid-level U.S. officers in the lift rather than simply people from Agence-France Press, or the BBC, even if this meant that he had to tape big *X*s on the windows at night to keep shards of glass from flying onto the bed during the B-40 rocket attacks. Billeting there also put him closer to the scene of the dark comedy. Every day at the Rex bar an American "diplomat" named Barry Zorthian, standing next to an army captain, would unveil the latest "body count" figures. These proved with mathematical certainty (thanks to the help of a giant Univac computer somewhere) that the United States was winning the war. The daily numbers were so obviously spurious that the reporters ran a pool: the person whose number came closest to Zorthian's wild projection won the jackpot. These briefings were known contemptuously as the "Five O'clock Follies."

Charles and I spent a good deal of time together when we were both living in Toronto.

"Every time I see you two characters together I think of James and his brother," a woman once told us.

She was an English prof, so Charles said, "Ah, yes, Henry and his brother William."

"No," she replied. "Jesse and Frank."

For indeed Charles and I rode together, so to speak, and raised some hell along the way.

So now that I was in Saigon, I made a point of putting up at the Rex, which seems not to have changed one bit from Charles's day. The lobby, the decor, the furniture — everything — was pure unadulterated 1965, neither retro nor preserved, but simply unaltered and unalterable. Staying there was like sleeping in Jackie Kennedy's rec room. I made repeated pilgrimages to the rooftop bar where over dinner with M I'd look out over the quiet city and propose toasts to Charles's memory.

— GONGS AND OTHER REMNANTS —

The first time I ever set foot in Saigon (many residents still don't call it Ho Chi Minh City), I was astonished to discover that I already knew my way around much of the city centre. How could that be? Was I experiencing déjà vu? No, it was simply that, like so many others of my generation, I once had been so deeply involved in the movement protesting the American War that my imagination had taken on some strange geographical understanding of the place that my contemporaries and I constantly read, wrote, talked, agonized, and obsessed about and just as often despaired of.

There, in Nguyen Hué Street, District 1, across the way from the Rex and right where I knew to expect it, was the former South Vietnam government's National Assembly. The French had built it as the Opera House, and these days it's known as the Municipal Theatre (where I was tempted to see a Saigon production of *Miss Saigon*). Next door: the Continental Hotel where much of Graham Greene's novel *The Quiet American* is set. And so on. Greene knew the Continental as being in the rue Catinat. During the American War the street became Tu Do — Freedom Street. After the war, it was changed again, to Dong Khoi — Uprising Street. In fact, it sometimes seems that most place-names in Vietnam have changed at least twice in my lifetime.

For the city and the country are made up of people who have moved on. I don't mean those who were too young to have known the war if indeed they were even alive. I don't mean only those who were adults during the war, with all its death, destruction, and hardship. I mean rather that the nation as a whole had shoved the entire period behind because that's what one does if one is Vietnamese. Through my subsequent stays there, I have come to admire their resilience. It is the kind of resilience that cannot be separated from patience and perseverance, though these qualities are mixed with anger.

An obvious symbol of this cocktail of stubborn virtues is the country's great military hero, General Vo Nguyen Giap, the hero of Dien Bien Phu, who, at the time of this writing, is still alive, age ninety-nine. His staggering victory was the dramatic conclusion to decades' worth of ambushes, bombings, skirmishes, harassments, and guerrilla actions. When, following the French withdrawal, the Americans decided to step in themselves and take on the self-commissioned task of defeating communism, the result was years of war between the northern Vietnamese on the one hand and southern Vietnamese, Americans, Australians, and New Zealanders on the other. The fight may have lasted until 1975, but its outcome became apparent to most everyone in 1968 when General Giap launched the brilliant Tet Offensive, breaking U.S. resolve. And it's well to remember that these Vietnamese who fought the French and Americans for a combined hundred years were the direct descendants of those who forcibly resisted the Chinese invaders for a *thousand* years — from our eighth century to the eighteenth. (And as we're constantly being told, a millennium is a long time in politics.)

The Vietnamese, northerners and southerners alike, know how to pull through, get by, and prosper. When I saw my friend Christopher Moore in Bangkok, he recalled:

> When I first went to Hanoi in 1990, everything was still pretty basic and grim. There were many bicycles on the streets, but very few private cars. The cars you did see weren't like the 1950s ones you found all over Havana, which the Cubans have kept in immaculate condition because there aren't any others to be had. The Vietnamese weren't restoring or rebuilding cars that way, they were *reinventing* them. When some vital piece of the engine broke down or actually fell off, they'd replace it with something from an old tractor, plough, lawn mower, or air conditioner: anything they could find to rig up. This made for some strangely unique vehicles. They looked like the crazy inventions in Rube Goldberg cartoons of

the 1920s and 30s. No, that's not right. What
they often looked like were the vehicles in the
Mad Max movies.

I think this leads to an important point. At the end of
the American War, large areas of the country were littered
with military detritus. Pieces of tanks, lorries, helicopters, and
winged aircraft, not to mention weapons, communications
equipment, and all the untold tonnes of other stuff necessary
to maintain in the field an army of, at its peak, half a million
people, seemed to be everywhere. One sees virtually no such
evidence today, apart from what's displayed as memorials —
for example, the partially submerged aircraft in Hanoi that
protrudes above the surface of what's called, in English, B-52
Lake (though it's actually a pond). The amount of American
war surplus that survives being almost infinitesimal, I'm always
a little surprised to discover, for example, metal boxes that
formerly held belts of .50-calibre machine-gun ammunition
being used by sidewalk shoeshine boys to carry their polishes,
rags, and brushes. For the Vietnamese turned nearly all abandoned war junk into scrap metal for export. Theirs is not a
melancholy or sentimental society, but rather a culture that
is always pulling itself up by what in this case could be called
their sandal-straps. Practical people, sometimes aggressively
so. Practical enough to also do a brisk trade in war nostalgia.

Not long after the war's conclusion, former U.S. service-
men began returning on nostalgic visits, if *nostalgic* is the correct word. They were generally well received by a forgiving
population. Two million Vietnamese had died in the war. The
survivors included one entire generation, possibly two, that
had come of age without much knowledge of how a market
economy operates. The government saw the great potential
in tourism, but worried that not enough U.S. dollars were

being spent on admission to such places as Saigon's Museum of Chinese and American War Crimes. I've never been able to confirm this, but my understanding is that the relevant government ministry hired consultants from the West. "Oh, now I see," I can hear top officials saying as they read the commissioned report. "If we desire their hard currency, we should not insult them to their faces — at least until they've bought a ticket." As a result, the institution is now called the War Remnants Museum. The transition involved no change to the exhibits, and it took place virtually overnight.

M was still doggedly pursuing her job of seeing how much French culture still lingered in Indochina. She was meeting with the director of the Maison de la Francophonie and even found someone who was visiting from France as a representative of the Association d'Amitié Franco-Vietnamienne. She charmed her way into the cozy flat of a welcoming, somewhat French-speaking, Vietnamese family. They lived in the artists' quarter around Notre-Dame Cathedral, whose priests, in a nod to Western travellers, have special permission to give short sermons in French and English after the regular service in Vietnamese. Our most interesting research discovery was that, unlikely as this sounds, the Rex had begun life as a storage garage for Renault motorcars.

We decided to visit the War Remnants Museum, supposing that even though only China and the U.S. had been mentioned in the original name, there just might be some displays on French war crimes, as well. Well, the museum does possess a guillotine that was used to dispatch captured Viet Minh insurgents in the 1940s. (There is another such instrument on display in Hanoi, at the old prison the French called Maison Centrale and the Americans knew as the Hanoi Hilton — thus confusing Saigon taxi drivers today who hear the phrase and try to drop off their American passengers at the new Hanoi Hilton Hotel, next to the Opera House.) Execution by guillotine ended in Indochina with the French withdrawal in 1954, but continued in France itself until 1977. Another exhibit referred to France at one remove. It was a representation of the so-called tiger cages, which people in the West may remember from the film *The Deer Hunter*. These little bamboo cages were used by both the Viet Cong and their enemies, though the model at the museum refers specifically to Viet Cong held on Côn Son Island, which the French, in one of their first acts after capturing Saigon, turned into a notorious prison for anti-colonial agitators. (It is now a resort, with a spa.)

Outside the War Remnants Museum sit restored American aircraft (how tiny the jet fighters of the 1960s seem), tanks, and other weapons. What's striking on the inside, horrifyingly so, are the photographs and other evidence of systemic American brutality in many forms. The museum is housed in what used to be the Saigon headquarters of the United States Information Agency, the same organization that ran the rooftop bar at the Rex as part of its propaganda effort. What the visitor sees on first entering is a glass case containing the medals and decorations donated by former Sergeant William Brown, late of the 173rd Airborne Brigade of the 503rd Infantry: a Silver Star, a Bronze Star, his wings and his marksman's decoration, a Purple Heart, and various others I couldn't identify. Brown has added a text: TO THE PEOPLE OF A UNITED VIETNAM. I WAS WRONG. I AM SORRY. His donation was a touching gesture. It has done so much to heal the maimed and restore the dead to life.

— TIDAL ACTIONS —

M and I weren't having any breakthroughs in terms of French culture in Vietnam. At one point I said, "Even Louisiana takes more pride in its French heritage!" If we were interested in just snapping pictures of more French-style buildings, we could have gone up Highway 20 to Dalat in the Central Highlands. This is a hill station (the very term puts the *Indo* in *Indochina*) to which the French would retreat at certain times of the year to escape the crippling heat down below. When most French nationals finally fled the city and the country, they left behind an estimated two thousand villas. Unfortunately, Dalat then reinvented itself as the honeymoon capital of Vietnam, coating itself in all the tacky charm of, say, Niagara Falls, Ontario, and Niagara Falls, New York. Suffice it to say that Dalat boasts a replica of the Tour Eiffel. Such is its reputation for the finer things in life that Dalat is also the name of perhaps the most popular brand of Vietnamese-made wine. The stuff tastes like poor quality grape juice, and its alcoholic content is so low as to be barely measurable; but it's cheap. So rather than explore the wine country, M and I followed the gorgeous coast of the South China Sea northward toward places whose names have a different resonance.

We came to Nha Trang (*Apocalypse Now*: "The generals back in Nha Trang would never believe this!"), and there we caught a break, or so we thought. We got invited to relax for a couple of days on a little island, two hours offshore by small boat, run by a French beachcomber-type. It is here, we were told, that Jacques-Yves Cousteau in the 1930s came up with the idea for the aqualung, which he and an engineer, who was his partner in the venture, developed shortly after the Second World War. The island is now being operated as a diving resort. In conversations at the six-stool bar, the proprietor would reveal little about his background in France beyond admitting that he had been in the military. The bar was made of thatch, like the scattering of huts and the open-sided dining area (the chef was French, as well). There was a pleasant little beach, complete with impossibly slim French women, topless, standing in the surf up to their knees, smoking cigarettes and talking, occasionally gesticulating with their long red fingernails. On my first venture into the sea I was savagely attacked, without provocation, by a sea urchin the size of the Sydney Opera House, and so hopped to safety on one foot, cursing mellifluously. A couple of days later, returning to the mainland with the French women and others, we were delayed by some malady involving the boat's motor. Departing way behind schedule, we thus arrived back on the mainland at low tide. We had to set up a kind of bucket brigade to move our luggage to dry land, passing it overhead from person to person, one piece at a time, as we slowly sank into the mud and sand.

We proceeded in a leisurely zigzag manner up the coast, passing the famous but not particularly impressive China Beach, and reached Hoi An, whose old quarter is another UNESCO World Heritage Site, like Luang Prabang, but whose reason for existing is bound up with trade rather than religion or royal politics. For centuries, before European colonialism reached full force (and before the river connecting it to the sea silted over), Hoi An was one of the most important ports in Southeast Asia and one of the most cosmopolitan. Arabs, Portuguese, and Dutch were numerous. So were the Japanese, until their culture entered its long period of hibernation in the seventeenth century. Such people were traders, merchants, sea captains — buyers and sellers (and transporters) of all sorts of goods. Many of them stayed seasonally, while others become permanent residents. The Chinese, however, had the largest presence in Hoi An, where they were treated respectfully and lived in peace. Chinese, including many direct descendants of the long-ago traders, still make up a sizable minority.

Hoi An has wisely banned automobiles in its old streets, which exude a sense of attentive decay. To make what first sounds like a ludicrous comparison, it's one of those cities, such as Venice, where you keep passing the unremarkable facades of private homes, wondering what treasures have lain inside for generations, even centuries. But it's a living community. M got up at five in the morning to witness the fish market, where she had been promised a virtual sea of women, standing and crouching over the day's catch, their conical straw hats, called *nón lá*, brim to brim almost as far as the eye could see.

"I wasn't disappointed," she said, exhaustedly, when we met up later at a little café we found at the end of a narrow lane. Its logo, puzzlingly, was the Boy Scout symbol, which the owner probably believes is a surefire way to attract Westerners. The place was an almost bare room with thick masonry walls, and so was quite cool.

The way Hoi An earns foreign exchange is through tailoring. No one can count the number of open-front shops filled with large bolts of real silk (and also "Vietnamese silk" or polyester), with tailors standing by to take the measurements of overseas visitors, even out on the pavement if necessary. They can whip up anything from pajamas to a ball gown or a smoking suit, sometimes in a few hours, but more often overnight. They can replicate any Western garment you might care to have cloned. They can even produce passable facsimiles of outfits pointed out to them in magazine adverts. To Westerners, the prices seem absurdly low — ten dollars, fifteen dollars — but of course the cost rises with the quality of the work. One can often tell a non-Vietnamese who's been to Hoi An for a day by the soft-looking square-cut shirt closed by toggles and with only the shortest stand-up collar. Like bolo neckties from Texas and turquoise cufflinks from Mexico, they begin to look ridiculous in the unforgiving daylight of one's natural habitat. They must linger in men's closets throughout Europe and the Americas.

It was nearly dusk the following day when we arrived at Danang, the place where the United States, after twenty years of covert interference in the region, finally launched its full-scale invasion of Vietnam. The first Marines came ashore here in the early spring of 1965. I find the timing significant because it coincides with the release of *Beach Blanket Bingo* in their cinemas back home. The beach at Danang is now very like an amusement park, with Ferris wheels and knick-knacks. Parasailing is popular where paratroopers strutted about in their big arrogant boots less than fifty years ago. I draw no special conclusions from this fact, except to remember that the tide comes in and the tide goes out again.

We headed north, over the Hai Van Pass, en route to Hué, stopping at some of the Cham towers. These brick sanctuaries are the most prominent physical reminders of the Champa kingdom, the society that flourished along this section of the coast for about 1,200 years. The Chams, who were prolific pirates, as well as builders, often found themselves at war with both the Khmers and the Vietnamese. The latter eventually overtook and completely metabolized them four centuries ago, but only after most Chams had become Hindus or, in a minority of cases, Muslims. This is yet another statement on how cosmopolitan this part of the country once was, with a brisk trade in ideas and beliefs as well as in goods.

Above the entrance to one of the temples was carved the familiar figure of a female Shiva, characteristic of Champa. Another temple was in easy sight of a much later structure: a large six-sided pillbox of poured concrete, with slit-like gun ports in the sides and a steel canopy on top to protect soldiers who once must have kept watch by peering over the rim. I wondered if this was an Army of the Republic of Vietnam position dating from the American War or possibly a leftover French construction? Somehow it looked quite French.

Even going at our own lazy pace, we soon slid into Hué, a magnificent city (another UNESCO World Heritage Site) whose survival has been imperilled so often by the same fact that makes it so interesting now. For it was the seat of the Nguyen Dynasty, which was established by the Emperor Gia Long in 1802 and lasted, in weakened condition, of course, until the close of the Second World War, when the last emperor, Bao Dai, stood on a belvedere and abdicated in favour of Ho Chi Minh's provisional government, whose out-and-out war against the French was just getting underway. As dynasties go, the Nguyen one did not have a long run, but it was certainly a transformative one. So much so that Nguyen is the family name of approximately half of the people in Vietnam. The mausoleums of the Nguyen rulers are spread out south of the city along a dozen or so kilometres. They are peaceful, as mausoleums should be. There are sculptures galore, including many one-third-life-size stone mandarins charged with handling the emperors' mundane daily affairs in the afterlife. One of the tombs is on a man-made lake so thickly covered in lily pads that you might suppose a green carpet had been laid down. It is best viewed from an elaborate wooden pavilion whose temple-style roof is decorated with huge bejewelled fish.

Hué's other attraction is its citadel, which is defined as a fortress built to protect a city (hence the term). In European usage, citadels often overlook the city from a high perch (as in, say, Quebec or Halifax). But the one that Gia Long built is on the same level as the community that it both surrounds and is itself surrounded by. It occupies an alluvial plain on the north bank of the Perfume River (whose beauties I recall Charles Taylor describing to me, though he saw the city at one of its unfortunate moments, when it had been besieged by U.S. and South Vietnamese troops). The citadel, which enclosed much of the civilian population as well as the Forbidden Purple City, accessible only to the emperor, his concubines, and his eunuchs, was reinforced by the French in the 1880s, following the rules of military geometry set down by the great Marquis de Vauban (1633–1707). The complex has ten huge gates, and the whole affair is surrounded by a moat. One corner of it is still known as the French Concession.

The citadel isn't an historical monument that has been left behind by modern history. On the contrary, during the Tet Offensive of 1968, it was captured by North Vietnamese regulars and Viet Cong guerrillas. The U.S. Marines were otherwise occupied at the time, under siege at Khe Sanh, not terribly far away, until General William Westmoreland, the most out-generaled general of the war, ordered U.S. and South Vietnamese troops to retake Hué regardless. Many people my age recall news footage of U.S. troops and CIA forces crouching behind one of the outside walls, unable to show themselves as they shot at the citadel by merely raising their M16s over the top and firing blindly. The Viet Cong ensign flew atop the flag tower for twenty-five days. About ten thousand people died at Khe Sanh, most of them communist troops. The same number, but mostly civilians, were killed at Hué, about a third of them by the occupying communists. Back in America, the ground seemed to have shifted under people's feet.

My most lasting impression of Hué is an odd one, perhaps, but also highly symbolic. M and I were taking a boat upriver to see where a bridge under construction would soon, alas, be eliminating the traditional ferry service. We passed part of the citadel where there were small, round sentry posts made of concrete, somewhat like miniatures of the multi-storey affair we had seen going over the pass. I couldn't get anyone to confirm that the French had left them, but such was my intuition. Later, I learned that the Vietnamese had recently turned them into public toilets. The genius of that! Here, located in the areas of busiest pedestrian traffic, were these private little kiosks, semi-subterranean and obviously almost indestructible, with slot-like firing holes high up near the roofs to provide good ventilation. There's something quintessentially Vietnamese in that idea.

Another and rather famous example of Vietnamese resilience can be seen in Hanoi. Back in the 1960s and early

The militarism that made French rule possible was another
lively visual topic. But images showcasing regular French troops
— such as this informal grouping of marsouins ("porpoises," a
slang term for common soldiers with long colonial service) are
unusual: everyone back home already knew what they looked like.
What sold were pictures of exotic natives in the service of France
— even the drum and bugle corps attached to a unit of tirailleurs
(the word can mean either "skirmishers" or "sharpshooters").

30. TONKIN - Hanoi — Cavalier annamite

P.DIEULEFILS.HANOI

This photo is especially evocative: the young Vietnamese cavalry-man has a fine pony, a crisp white uniform, a polished sabre — but no shoes.

3130 TONKIN — Tribunal indigène - Le prisonnier à genoux d...

Punishment is another theme of postcards from Indochina. The photo of a Vietnamese prisoner pleading before a local tribunal is cautionary, but not particularly frightening, even though the young man on the far left carries a crossbow. In contrast, gruesome images of decapitated prisoners were always popular.

TONKIN

48. Têtes de Pirates Chinois

767. TONKIN — Bảo-Lạc
Partisan Mèo tenant une tête de Pirate

*Here a Hmong (*Mèo *in Vietnamese,* Miao *in Chinese) working for the French exhibits the head of an executed "pirate": as in China, a generic term for a bandit or ideological opponent, not necessarily one who commits crimes at sea. In keeping with local practice (*"selon la coutume du pays"*), such pirates' heads were often put on display, hanging from city walls in baskets or open boxes, accompanied by a written warning from the authorities. In districts closest to China and Burma, crucifixion was another common punishment.*

Colonial Laos was less well developed than Vietnam and Cambodia, and this fact was reflected in its postcard iconography. There are fewer scenes of urban life, but proportionately more showing village people, both Lao and members of the ethnic minorities; French faces are rarely glimpsed.

Some images, such as the one that records a gathering of elephant wallahs, are strikingly specific to a distant past. But photos of a local boat race, and one of small passenger and cargo vessels tied up near Luang Prabang, have a more contemporary feel, for much of Lao life still focuses on the Mekong and its tributaries.

Postcards such as this one of a kerbside dealer in soya cheese or the crowds always to be found at Binh Tay Market in Cholon, the city's Chinatown, remind us that colonial Saigon, like all important Asian cities, was a constant whirl of small-scale commerce. But it was also one on which the French would put their grand and indelible stamp, to remind the world who was in charge.

In the years bridging the nineteenth and twentieth centuries, French neoclassical buildings, some of them inspired by particular Parisian examples, changed the face of Saigon. The Palais du Gouverneur Général de l'Indochine (top), built in 1902, but shown here in 1925, almost reeked of power. Since 1975, the building has been known as the Reunification Palace. Other French structures have retained their original functions. The custom house (middle) is still the custom house. The main post office (bottom; its famous glass dome obscured by trees in this 1920s postcard) also continues to serve its intended purpose.

No doubt inspired in a small way by Baron Georges-Eugène Haussmann, whose development scheme had redrawn the map of Paris during the Second Empire, a generation earlier, the colonial authorities remade the plat of Saigon by creating majestic avenues. One street that required no such reinvention was the Boulevard Bonnard, named for Jean-Louis Bonnard, a Catholic priest executed by Emperor Tu Duc in 1852 (and later canonized). Instead, the French decorated it with important buildings, private and public. One was the Opera House, which much later, after the country was partitioned in 1954, became the National Assembly of the American-backed Republic of South Vietnam. It is now the city's municipal theatre. The boulevard has been renamed Le Loi Street, after the Vietnamese general who defeated the Chinese six hundred years ago.

Beginning in 1802, Hué, located on the Perfume River about midway between Saigon and Hanoi, was the seat of the Nguyen emperors. It is now the site of their elaborate tombs.

The French took Hué by force in 1885, looting the palace. But they permitted the monarchy to survive, at least nominally, until 1945.

Accordingly, most colonial-era postcards of the city detail court life, with its retainers, attendants, and its various ceremonies and celebrations. The city, with its famous citadel, was the scene of fierce fighting during the Tet Offensive of 1968.

117 — Une Bonzesse annamite
de la Cour de Hué

Missionnaire en pirogue (Tonkin)   A boating missionary (Tonkin)

This missionary on his way to evangelize the Tonkinese is a reminder that the impulses behind the French mission civilatrice *were Christian as well military, political, and commercial. Hanoi became the most heavily Roman Catholic city in Indochina, but Buddhism, of course, remained the dominant belief system, there and throughout most of Asia.*

Before and after the colonial period, just as during it, Hanoi certainly had its earthy aspects, but also enjoyed a large middle class of cultured Vietnamese. Private citizens, for example, financed the bridge, shown here on a 1920s postcard, that connects central Hanoi to Nogoc Son Temple, on a tiny island in Hoan Kiem Lake.

23. TONKIN - Haïphong — Port de Commerce

Until relatively recent years, only one bridge connected Hanoi to Haiphong, its vital seaport. Designed by the famous Gustave Eiffel, the railway and auto span, completed in 1902, stretches 2,500 metres across the Red River. It was named the Pont Paul Doumer, to honour the governor general of Indochina from 1897–1902 (who later, in 1931, became president of France— until assassinated the following year). In post-colonial times, the Vietnamese renamed it the Long Bien Bridge. During the American War of 1965–75, U.S. bombers destroyed the bridge repeatedly, only to see the Vietnamese rebuild it again and again.

1970s, only one bridge, the Long Bien span across the Red River, linked the city with Haiphong, its vital seaport. The bridge was designed (by Gustave Eiffel no less) for rail traffic as well as foot and vehicular use. It is 2,500 metres long and looks like a giant Erector Set construction. Between 1965 and 1975, it was attacked numerous times by American warplanes intent on cutting off Hanoi's food supplies. The bombers concentrated on the centre sections, which would crash into the deepest part of the channel. They went so far as come up with new types of bombs for this purpose. But each time the bridge was attacked, the Vietnamese rebuilt it, sometimes using American prisoners as part of the labour gangs to ensure the repairs would go ahead without interruption — only to be knocked down again. In this story, many people see confirmation of the view that the Vietnamese are realistic, pragmatic, and pugnaciously businesslike people: apostles of the doable.

I've mentioned earlier in certain parts of central Vietnam, where the Americans used the same sort of carpet bombing as they did in Laos, residents have incorporated the craters into their irrigation system with enough ingenuity to give themselves an extra crop of rice. It is as though they said to themselves, "The gods have given us all these free holes. How can we turn them to good account?" I'm also thinking of one of the famous places to eat in Hanoi, a family-run restaurant called Cha Cha La Vong, located in an old building at the top of a gruelling flight of worn wooden stairs. It serves only one dish, made from whatever fish the family has caught that day, prepared *cha cha* style, ground and highly seasoned. The dish has given its name to Cha Cha Street, which is now full of other establishments of the same type. When eating in one of these places I chanced to admire the little altar on the wall honouring the owner's ancestors. Beside the customary incense, paper offerings, and fresh oranges, was an unopened bottle of Mekong Whisky. I enjoyed the meal so much that I returned the following evening. Everything was just the same except that the whisky bottle was now only half full.

As I say, an immensely practical people.

⊰ ☀ ⊱

— DOWNPOUR —

M and I made our way to Hanoi both knowing that as I will never be able to write as well as the English traveller A.A. Gill, I could at least quote him. "If the opposite of love isn't hate but indifference," he has said of Vietnam, "the opposite of war isn't peace; it's prosperity." For more than a decade, the Vietnamese economy had been growing by as much as 10 percent annually. In such a young and busy population, focused on this day and the next, we were actually surprised to find some throwbacks to the wartime period almost as soon as we arrived, such as my being offered marijuana or the services of "boom-boom girls."

Every day we gingerly crossed boulevards, sidestepping crowds of Vietnamese women on motor scooters. They had on the traditional *ao dai*, those silk dresses worn over trousers and slit up both sides. When putting along in heavy traffic through the polluted streets, they also wear masks over their mouths and what look very much like eighteen-button opera gloves. One day when I reached the other side, I bumped into a fellow who I thought was pulling a switchblade on me. In fact, he was an innocent knife vendor demonstrating his wares only a step or two from my throat, though this wasn't immediately apparent as he didn't have his tray of knives in front of him, but kept it under one arm where I didn't quite see it for what it was. There was a tense moment until I figured out what was happening. And shortly afterwards we saw something wonderful.

We had taken what looked like the maid's quarters in a small hotel in the Old Quarter: a minuscule slot-like room with a teak floor, under the eaves five storeys up, one more than was serviced by the lift. We had just left the lobby for the extreme hubbub outside when suddenly the street sellers began gathering up their goods and disappearing somewhere. In what seemed an instant, they were gone, and their potential customers with them. Believing that this indicated simply that the day's instalment of the torrential rain was set to begin, we naively thought people were over-reacting, even as leaves, twigs, and other debris started to swirl about the empty inter-section as though trapped in a wind tunnel. Being sensible Vancouverites, we went back upstairs for our umbrellas. Before we even reached the room, the sky was as dark as though in a total eclipse. A great tropical storm was well underway.

We stood in our rickety lodging overlooking perhaps two centuries' worth of red-tiled rooftops as gale-force winds came from the west, blowing the rain in such a way as to send it speeding up the streets, which soon flooded. Antennae — bamboo and even steel — toppled off roofs into the lanes below. Tarpaulins rudely torn from one building became tangled in another. Windows shattered. The most amazing feature was the way that the thick curtain of fast-moving rain obscured all the luxury joint-venture hotels and other high-rise construction in the distance. All evidence of the city's new wealth was blacked out. What was left looked like a Doré engraving of Paris illustrating a work by Victor Hugo. For the couple of hours the storm lasted, we were transfixed by the unexpected glimpse of what nineteenth-century Hanoi must have looked like. This was as close as we had come thus far to understanding that there *is* still a French atmosphere in Hanoi, as the tourist authorities always insist.

The streets round St. Joseph's Cathedral, for example, are described as a lingering expression of the old colonial culture, but time and again we were disabused of the notion that the francophone heritage we were seeking actually exists. In practical day-to-day terms, the greatest experience of French culture that M and I had come upon in Hanoi was a pair of backpacking Québécoises living in the same run-down pension as ourselves. They were travelling together. Although not related, they were identically dressed, and identically tattooed and pierced from top to toe, and were both named Véronique. This naturally led to confusion that seemed uproarious at the time, especially to them.

The storm ended as abruptly as it began, and we went looking for a place to have a congenial drink. We found a jazz club where a four-piece Vietnamese band — tenor sax, bass, keyboard, and drums — was working itself into quite a lather while waiters slithered up to all the little round tables with trays of intimate antiquarian cocktails such as Sidecars and White Russians. I remember that the music, too, was attractively of a certain period, as though we had time-travelled back to classical modernism. It was the kind of nightclub where you could ask the bandleader, in almost-correct French, *"Est-ce que vous connaissez le 'Muskrat Ramble'?"* and the answer would be yes.

Yet I could not quite place the familiar-sounding melody line running beneath what the saxophonist had been pounding out for the past twenty minutes or so. It would have come to me, but my concentration was broken by what I believed might be incipient violence. Two tables away, in another throwback moment, sat an obvious example of the former American military man returned on a mission of exorcism and nostalgia, what I have heard the Vietnamese call a *vietnamman*, all one word. He was about sixty-five, bull-necked, with a white buzzcut, and must have been drinking much of the afternoon. His heckling of the musicians became so loud that the sax player was no longer able to drown it out. He was, it seemed to me, only one Scotch away from standing up and screaming some imprecation about dog-eatin' sonsabitches. I thought I'd better get M out of there and myself with her.

Later that night, as I lay sleepless in the garret room, the name of the tune suddenly came to me. Was it Ellington? Was it Basie? No, it was the theme music from *The Flintstones*.

— THE MAN IN THE GLASS COFFIN —

Many of Ho Chi Minh's enemies could not help but admire him. One example is William J. Duiker, an American diplomat who served in the U.S. Embassy in Saigon and then devoted thirty years to writing a highly sympathetic Ho biography. Another is Jean Sainteny, a French official charged with negotiating with Ho on terms for ending the Franco-Indochinese war. He praised Ho as an "ascetic man, whose face revealed at once intelligence, energy, cleverness, and finesse …" That seemed to me a pretty accurate description of how Ho looks in death, lying in his mausoleum in Hanoi. I have seen the preserved bodies of two of the other three communist leaders that were put on display this way, as patriotic shrines, but also as evidence of Russian embalming prowess. But neither Lenin's corpse nor Mao's conveys the humanity of Ho's. (I can't pass a judgment on the body of Stalin, who used to share space with the dead Lenin, but was then removed to a simple slot in the Kremlin wall.)

Ho was born in 1890, seven years before Conchinchina, Annam, Tonkin, Laos, and Cambodia were finally united under the official name Indochine Française. He died in 1969, the year that President Lyndon Johnson, knowing he couldn't win re-election while also losing the war in Vietnam, announced that he would quit politics and return to his ranch. Between the bookends of these two dates one can read the story of one of the twentieth century's most extraordinary lives.

Ho was born Nguyen Sinh Cung. When he was ten, however, his parents changed his name to Nguyen Tat Thanh ("Nguyen the Accomplished") when his father, a poor Confucian scholar, became the first person in his district to earn a doctorate. Ho had two siblings, a brother who was geomancer and a sister who was a clerk for the French military. Their father knew French as well as Chinese. To support the family, he accepted trivial posts in the colonial civil service, but did so with the utmost reluctance, for he despised French rule, which had become ever harsher during his lifetime.

Like his father, Ho was of scholarly temperament and had a great gift for languages. At seventeen, he graduated from the most prestigious French-language school in Vietnam, the Quoc Hoc, or National Academy. In time he also became proficient in English, Russian, Japanese, and Czech, as well as in three Chinese languages and an unknown number of Annamite dialects. During the American War, President Ho forsook the idea of occupying the former governor general's palace in Hanoi, but lived nearby, in a small stilted house that is today a memorial and museum. There is one tiny bedroom, almost bare of furniture or ornament, and a somewhat larger room dominated by a meeting table with eleven chairs. Important personages from elsewhere in Asia and abroad would call on him there. One day he received a representative from Germany, and astonished his young aides by conducting a long conversation in fluent German, a language they had no idea he knew. But then as a professional revolutionary, determined to give his country back to the Vietnamese people, he was of necessity a man of many secrets.

At first his resistance to French rule was passive, but later, in Hué, he participated in a coup attempt organized by a well-established nationalist group. The leader and others were arrested, but Ho, now a fugitive, hid in a remote hamlet on the coast where he taught classical French literature in Chinese.

Later he slipped down to Saigon, struggling to remain inconspicuous in a series of menial jobs, but finally he had to flee. He signed on to work in the galley of the steamer *Admiral Latouche-Tréville*, bound for Marseilles. He was twenty-one years old. But his first stay in France was brief, as he knew he dare not linger and so found passage to the United States. He worked variously as a labourer and a household servant, subsequently finding employment at a famous American hotel, the Parker House in Boston. He became interested in the plight of African-Americans, joining the activists of the Universal Negro Improvement Trust and travelling to the southern states, where he was horrified to witness a lynching. But then much in America and in France horrified him, particularly a level of urban poverty he had never experienced in Vietnam. He found another ship and worked his way to London. His experience in ships' galleys was sufficient to secure him a dishwashing job at the Carlton Hotel. There he impressed himself upon the famous restaurateur Auguste Escoffier, known as *"le roi des cuisiniers et cuisinier des rois"* who taught him how to be a pastry chef. The profession suited him well while he studied Marx in the off-duty hours.

When the Great War erupted, Ho ran toward it, returning to France, where he set himself up as a professional photographer in Montmartre, joined the Socialist Party, contributed to radical newspapers, wrote a play, became addicted to American cigarettes, and changed his name to Nguyen Ai Quoc ("Nguyen the Patriot"). After the war, he composed a manifesto calling for Vietnamese independence. He tried to deliver it at the Versailles peace conference, but was turned away at the gate, even though he was wearing a claw-hammer coat borrowed from one of his bohemian friends. The National Assembly also denied him admittance. One of the progressive newspapers printed his demands as a pamphlet and distributed it throughout Paris. The document provoked a scandal whose effects were certainly felt in Hanoi, as well, and led Ho to undertake a European speaking tour. From that point on, he was forever on the minds of the French secret service.

In 1923, as a rather unorthodox student of Marxism, Ho entered university in Moscow where he was instructed in strategy, propaganda, and political organization. He met Lenin, Trotsky, and Bukharin, as well as some famous fellow foreigners, Chiang Kai-shek and Zhou Enlai (who were not yet each other's adversaries). With his extraordinary capacity for impressing people, he became a protégé of Mikhail Borodin, the legendary spy and agitator. Borodin had travelled the world in the service of the Comintern, or Third International, charged with fomenting communism wherever he went. He had already completed long assignments in the United States (where he was known as "Mike Gruzenberg"), Britain, Scandinavia, and Mexico, and now was being sent to China. He took Ho with him to Canton to organize Vietnamese communists exiled there. But Ho's interest lay entirely with the cause of Vietnamese independence, not with that of international communism as such, and he made another recruiting and speech-making tour of Europe, covering his tracks as usual. In 1928, he turned up in Thailand, posing as a Buddhist monk, to organize expat Vietnamese there. (By that time, Borodin's career had taken an unfortunate turn. The previous year, Chiang Kai-shek had shown his true colours and massacred communists in Shanghai. Borodin had to flee, escaping to Russia by motorcycle across the Gobi Desert; he died in 1951 in one of Stalin's Siberian prison camps.)

I knew the basic outlines of Ho's story as M and I looked through the glass sarcophagus at his remains. In 1930, he went to China once more, to reinvigorate the Vietnamese Communist Party from Hong Kong. He nearly died of tuberculosis in a British prison the next year. But then, once free, he simply disappeared. There were unconfirmed sightings of him in places as far apart as East Africa and Indonesia. Some reports suggested he was travelling under entirely new aliases, such as Nguyen O Phap, Nguyen Sihh Chin, Song Man Tcho, and Ly Thuy. Just as there are seven missing years in Shakespeare's life, so there are ten in Ho's — until he suddenly turned up back in Vietnam in 1941, astonishing all those who had heard he was dead, and set about building an umbrella organization of all the anti-French and anti-Japanese factions. For the Nazis had installed a puppet Vichy government in Indochina. It was at this point that Nguyen Vo Giap, wearing a homburg, appeared in Ho's jungle clearing. He was a former Hanoi high school history teacher whose father died in one of the French colonial prisons, and he agreed to form a Vietnamese army. At the beginning there were thirty-one male recruits and three female ones. One year later, with Ho and Giap organizing, the combined total was more than ten thousand. The Office of Strategic Services, the U.S. intelligence presence in the area, kept refusing to supply the Vietnamese with arms or money to harass the Japanese. But once Ho began rescuing downed American pilots and getting them safely back into American hands, the position changed slightly: He was given half a dozen revolvers and twenty thousand rounds of ammunition. It was a start.

— A BROKEN JOURNEY —

M and I had to get back to Saigon and thence to Canada. As this was the time of year when students were travelling en masse, there was no room on the famous Reunification Express, which has been running non-stop (a forty-hour journey) between Hanoi and Saigon since 1976, three years before Paul Theroux wrote about it so grumpily *The Great Railway Bizarre*. We would have to make our way by stages — a couple of big leaps if possible, rather than several smaller ones. The prospect was not entirely unpleasant. As Vietnam is a tall, skinny country, virtually all its trains (like Chile's) run on a north-south axis and usually come with a view of the sea at least part of the way. Also, the fares are quite low. Prices fluctuate, but let's put it this way: if you can stand to sit in a noisy jam-packed coach the entire way (as we were not — not this time), you can theoretically travel almost a thousand kilometres for seventy-five thousand dong, about five U.S. dollars, at least in the cheaper monsoon season when the temperatures get damn close to forty degrees except during the couple of hours a day when rain comes down hard enough to wash out roads.

So it was that we were on the overnight train to Hué. It was made up of eleven passenger coaches painted Soviet railway green and one nearly paintless freight car, pulled by a bright red diesel locomotive. The passage of 850 kilometres was scheduled to take twelve and a half hours. That isn't a poor showing given that that the train, nominally an express, isn't especially fast. Vietnam's narrow-gauge track limits speed and the train frequently slows and even stops dead for significant periods, waiting on sidings for slightly quicker ones to pass.

For a socialist society, Vietnam maintains a perplexing class system on its trains. Despite Highway 1, the coast road going the whole length of the country, trains are still the primary means of moving people and stuff between the south and the north. During the French and American wars, both insurgents and Westerners were forever trying to sabotage rail traffic in each other's sectors. The Viet Minh and later the Viet Cong proved effective at this, planting agents within the workforce at key points. For today's traveller, the basic distinctions are between coach seats and berths on the one hand and between Hard and Soft on the other. In the simplest possible terms, you could say that coach passengers sit and berth people recline, that Hard tickets imply sleeping fans while Soft suggests air con. In practice, the matter is more complicated, particularly as regards population density, food quality, and basic hygiene. For this first leg of our discontinuous trip down the length of Vietnam, M and I were going Soft berth, top of the line.

In the commotion of settling in and preparing to get under way, a Vietnamese woman poked her head in to ask if her child could come look at the foreigners. We willingly obliged. The compartments are designed like those on old European trains and decorated in washroom green. One difference between a first-class sleeper and a second is that the former has a large window. Whereas in second class all you see from an upper berth is the blur of grass and the ends of railway ties, in the first-class equivalent you can look out at the life you are passing. All through Hanoi and its suburbs, houses and shops extend to the edge of the right-of-way. As the train slowly rattled past, we saw families in their nightclothes watching television. Even in Hanoi, however, the sprawl has an outer edge, and well before we ourselves were ready for lights-out we were deep in a rural reality.

Vietnamese trains move much like the geckos you some-times find onboard. They lie deceptively still, resting and perhaps thinking. Then they frantically dart across a short distance. The process is repeated at intervals so irregular that their enemies in the wild can never predict their movements. Between major cities the rail timetables are crowded. At any given moment there's always a southbound train, designated by *S* and two or three digits, or a northbound one, with the *N* prefix, leaving in thirty minutes or so. In earlier days, the stations were full of hissing steam engines, like the one built in 1945 that is pre-served outside the station in Danang. Steam locomotives are still used sometimes for freight, especially for shunting round the yards, as in China. Cambodia was the last place I was aware of that had used steam to move passengers.

Although the Vietnamese engines are relatively up to date, some of the rolling stock is fascinatingly decrepit. It looks even more so when it's burdened by overcrowding at peak times. In the parlour cars, passengers often stand or sit in the aisles and hang out the windows. In the Pullman cars, large numbers of Vietnamese, previously unacquainted with one another, share berths, two and even three to a narrow one-person bed. The trains were especially crowded when we were there. Yes, because so many students were barging up and down the countryside.

A distressing feature of the trains is the Vietnamese pop music piped throughout. Occupants of individual compartments can turn it down and sometimes off in their own spaces, but the noise spills over from the corridors, leaving the air as heavily sound-polluted as before. The stuff is kept on for hours after sensible people have dropped off to sleep. It comes on again at 0530 or 0600 hours at the latest, blasting everyone back to wakefulness. Only for a few hours during the night are the songs turned off. This is perverse, because it ensures that no one will be awake to enjoy the comparative peacefulness of these interludes.

In the darkness somewhere, we passed Dong Ha and the Ben Hai River, the boundary between North and South Vietnam imposed by the Geneva Accord of 1954. The famous Demilitarized Zone (DMZ) was reckoned from an imaginary line drawn down the centre of the river. When U.S. forces supplanted French ones, the DMZ became heavily militarized indeed. To the extent that the American War had battle lines at all, this is where the American front lines were, facing the river, looking north to the origin of the Ho Chi Minh Trail, with which so much U.S. policy was concerned. That morning when the speakers came on and threw us out of bed, cursing, we had to scramble to get our gear together and get off the train, which was stopped at Hué's station for only a few minutes.

After waiting in Hué for a day or more, we were about to resume the southbound trip by getting to Nha Trang. We realized we were in for a dispiriting time when our train simply didn't show up. Other trains, with later departure times shown on the timetable, came and went, and we were left shifting our weight from foot to foot. Enquiring elicited nothing because we don't speak a word of Vietnamese, but also because railway personnel seem to believe that the schedule is a divine reality, not an estimate or a guideline, subject to revision. To question the schedule is simply not done; to point out, politely, that the schedule may be mistaken is to transgress some inviolable etiquette. Through intermediaries, we finally learned that our train was late because the whole affair had been expropriated by the army. Sure enough, the station began filling with officers dripping with braid and carrying cheap plastic briefcases full of relevant paperwork. Once their documents were processed, their train, which I suspect had been loitering just out of sight on a siding, slunk into view, sheepishly, I thought. It quickly departed with a full load of mid-level personnel, for this was neither a VIP train nor a troop train, but something in between, bound where and for what purpose we couldn't tell. Ours followed, even more shamefacedly, in about an hour and a half. It was a poor substitute.

For one thing, it was second class. The locomotive was identical to the one on our original Hanoi train, but the carriages were even more battered. They were more primitive-looking somehow, with metal grilles in the windows instead of glass. Even out on the platform, the smell from inside the carriages got into our nostrils. It was dark now, and the night promised to be a long one. Our assigned compartment was the nearest one to the squat toilet. We weren't certain whether this was a plus or a minus. Because the spaces in the grilles were big enough to admit a small hand, we had to sleep with our feet facing the windows and stash all our gear up by our heads, using our spare clothes as pillows.

We were sharing a compartment with a young English couple. When the male half, who had drawn the lower bunk, sat down, he noticed insects that seemed to resent the intrusion. He got up and pulled back the thin mattress to find the wooden surface underneath alive with bug life. He went off, bracing himself against the bulkheads of the pitching car, to find someone to complain to, but returned only with a fresh set of bed linen, recently washed, but still greasy to the touch. He settled in for a while, but grumbled loudly. Then he hit on the idea of climbing up top, to pass the journey with his girlfriend (as though her bed wasn't infested — he must have reasoned that the insects weren't the climbing or flying varieties). As I lay there in the top berth across from them, feeling relatively secure (M and I had done as the guidebooks suggest and brought our own sheets in which to wrap ourselves), I couldn't help seeing them facing each other in the lotus position, playing cards. I dozed off for a bit and when I woke, the friendly hand of cards had turned to foreplay. I tried to get back to sleep. For various reasons, this wasn't easy.

In the slot-like aisle between the two tiers of beds was an all-purpose table. It was supposed to lie flat against the wall until needed, when a hook could be unlatched to let it swing out and a leg would descend to support it. The latch was broken and the damn thing banged against the wall at every curve in the track, however slight. I tried everything I could think of to fix it, including padding the underside with clothing to deaden the noise and stacking all the backpacks on the floor underneath to keep it in the fully extended position. Nothing worked. What's more, people kept barging into the compartment unannounced: cops with red collar-tabs and high-peaked caps, conductors demanding to see our tickets once again, hawkers selling really dreadful food at exorbitant prices. M and I arrived somewhat bedraggled after yet another twelve-hour trip.

Days passed before we were willing to risk train travel again, and by then our luck, it seemed, had turned. We were ready to take the train from Nha Trang to Saigon. This time, the hours weren't quite so gruelling. The train was intended to arrive at 0400 hours after departing at about dinner time. Here we learned a valuable lesson. There's a point beyond which it doesn't matter what category of ticket you buy. What matters is the age and condition of the train, which is purely a question of the luck of the draw. This time the cars were clean and the compartment had once been decorated and instead of Vietnamese pop tunes we got a documentary — not too long — about the history of Saigon. The colour scheme was a bluish mauve. There was glass in the window and curtains over the glass.

Only once did things look as though they might turn on us. M had the top bunk and I was in the other top one, across from her. Down below were two New Zealanders who didn't come in until late, as they were off partying in another coach. Behind M's head when she lay down was a luggage storage area with double doors. One of the doors kept working its way loose and gently banging her on the skull. Remembering the table from hell, I tried several times to tie the two door handles together, using, for example, one of my bootlaces; nothing would hold. She was about to sleep facing the other way, with feet instead of her head in the line of danger, when an idea struck me: a condom. I got out the only one I had and knotted it tightly around the handles. It gave a bit on sharp bends but was elastic enough to spring right back into place, silently. The fact that it was the lubricated kind made it easy to tie as emergency hardware, though, as I might have foreseen, this also meant that it gradually worked its way loose as we slept. When this happened and the doors flung themselves open, striking M on the cranium, the condom flew up in the air and landed, we thought, on or in the sleeping bag of the Kiwi woman down below. While I held the doors together manually, M had to inquire of the not-yet-quite-asleep fellow passenger. "Excuse me," she said. "Our condom seems to have come loose. I think it might have gone into your bedding. Would you mind checking for us, please?

"Bugger!" said the New Zealander. "Now I've heard everything."

I was mugged by the realization that we had just become the travel story she'd be telling people back home in Auckland. Fortunately, she didn't know our names.

Noel Coward said that the melody and lyrics of "Mad Dogs and Englishmen" just "popped into my head" during a trip from Hanoi to Saigon. Of course, he was travelling by motorcar, not train.

— CRACKS IN THE EMPIRE —

Time passed. I had returned to Southeast Asia, alone once again. M's fluency in French hadn't got us terribly far. The search for Frenchness in Indochina, and Vietnam in particular, had become increasingly ridiculous: an endless cycle of half-baked inference. I had sought out the places where the concept of French Indochina originated. I had poked among the fragile ruins of French culture in the places where it once had flourished. The narrative I was seeking didn't really seem to exist; there was nothing but its highly dramatic ending.

So I got in touch with Christopher Moore and asked if he wanted to travel with me to Dien Bien Phu where the French were driven out of Asia once and for all. I didn't have

to use much persuasion, as I knew that this was one of the
few places in the region he hadn't visited. What's more, he
had always wanted to talk with the so-called Black Thai, a
distinct cultural group who have lived near the Lao border for
uncounted generations, remote from the Thais of Thailand
from whom they descend. They speak an odd variant of the
standard Thai that Christopher was eager to see if he could
understand. Emails flew between his base in Bangkok and
mine in Vancouver as we ironed out the details. I would go
to Hanoi and settle in there for a while, waiting for his arrival
when he had an opening in his writing schedule.

Hanoi has serious traffic and pollution problems and
some truly ugly suburbs — which megalopolis does not? —
but at its centre, frequent wars notwithstanding, remains the
stately and refined city it has so long proclaimed itself to be.
To put the matter in Western terms, Hanoi is to Saigon as
Montreal is to Toronto and Melbourne is to Sydney: less
brash and materialistic and certainly more cultured — and
sensitive about its loss of power. For heaven's sake, it has a
Temple of Literature.

Travelling light and solo, I went straight from the airport
to the northern part of the city and holed up there with pleas-
ure, shifting from one small hotel to another as the rates rose
or fell according to the occupancy levels. I did a good deal of
walking in the Thirty-Six Streets, an area I imagine probably
reminds American visitors of Greenwich Village, though it's
both more charming and more alive. The old guild system
that assigned silk merchants, salt sellers, and birdcage makers
to particular streets is long gone, and the artisanal proportion
of the population is always shrinking. Yet among the temples
with swallow-tail roofs and all the clubs, bars, restaurants, and
souvenir stands (the nearly instantaneous result of the *doi moi*,
the economic liberalization that began in 1986), it's still possible to pick up the tinware one might need in Hang Thiec

Street and shop in Hang Ma for all manner of paper goods, including those used as votive offerings. On one walk, when I had only my reading glasses, not my distance ones, I looked up to see a richly colourful outdoor flower market in the distance. When I got closer I realized that, no, those weren't flowers, but rather motorbike helmets of every conceivable shade and finish, hundreds and hundreds of them, possibly a thousand or two, hanging on pegboards affixed to a shop front.

For exercise I walked everyday round Hoan Kiem Lake, with its graceful little bridge leading to a temple in the middle. One day I was resting from these mild cardio exertions by Hoa Phong Tower. This is a squat two-storey brick affair with its name in traditional Chinese characters. It is open on the sides and the interior walls are covered over in lovers' graffiti. Suddenly I was nuzzled by a Great Dane — a Harlequin, the largest of that breed. The dog's owner was a pleasant American woman in her thirties. As Great Danes (and old men such as myself) require a great deal of exercise, she, I, and the dog kept running into one another, and sometimes sat on a bench, chatting. She had been living in Hanoi for a year and had two more to go before being rotated home. "My husband works at the embassy," she explained. I dearly wanted to ask a simple factual question about American diplomacy in Vietnam, but didn't know how to do so without running the risk of appearing impolite. I wanted to ask: Where are embassy personnel down in Saigon put up, given that the Pittman Building was torn down long ago, as though to erase a shameful memory? The Pittman was the apartment block on the embassy grounds from whose rooftop people were rescued by helicopter and ferried to naval vessels offshore on April 30, 1975, the day the Americans lost the war.

A common observation about Hanoi is that it shows so few traces of the American War. Few physical traces at any rate, rather than psychic ones. The cliché is rendered all the truer by a handful of vivid exceptions. The centre section of the city's magnificent nineteenth-century railway station was destroyed in the infamous Christmas Day Bombing of 1972, a fact made unforgettable even to tourists by the way that the missing part was rebuilt in the Soviet brutalist style. But what's most remarkable is not the amount of evidence of the American War, but the nearly complete absence of any from the long war against the French. Although northern Vietnam was fed largely by the labour of southern Vietnam, Hanoi was the administrative seat of all French Indochina. It was at the centre of a textbook closed-market system, in which the colonies were obliged to sell the French their crops and minerals cheaply while being forced to pay dearly for the mandatory importation of French manufactured goods. Not coincidentally, Hanoi and the north more generally were also the scene of most of the unrest that often broke out as insurgency.

Throughout the 1930s, young radical intellectuals engaged in subtle acts of sabotage — and other acts not so subtle. The Second World War left the situation confused and even more complicated, but once it was over, the nationalist movement surged. Looking today at the Hanoi Opera House, on whose steps newlyweds are often photographed, one has no sense of the fighting that took place there. At the former governor general's residence, there are only a few pockmarks in an iron railing to remind people of the pitched battle fought there in August 1945 — the month before Ho stood in Ba Dinh Square (a space long since Sovietized in appearance) and read aloud the new republic's founding document, which he had drafted in a house at 48 Hang Ngang. He called this instrument the Declaration of Independence, and plagiarized liberally from the American one of the same name.

But Hanoi was still at war, and the French were able to bring it to the threshold of starvation by cutting it off from the south. In 1947, the French recaptured the city, and people's suffering became deeper and more widespread as the urban warfare grew more intense and deadly. Natives pointed me to traffic-choked intersections, places without commemorative markers, where ambushes and bombings had once taken place. There are said to have been spies and counter-spies in every neighbourhood; in some neighbourhoods, in every street; in some streets, on every block. Citizens who could do so fled to the countryside, which was the Viet Minh's base of support. Some suggest that by 1948 or 1949 there were only about ten thousand civilians still living in Hanoi. Following Dien Bien Phu, the Viet Minh retook the city — easily, as the French were taking flight — and in a few years the population had climbed to four hundred thousand. But it was a fundamentally different place, not merely bigger. In what seemed to the twentieth-century West a practical way to behave, the United Nations partitioned Vietnam. There would now be two Vietnams just as there were two Germanys and two Koreas: the communist Democratic Republic of Vietnam in the north, the capitalist Republic of Vietnam in the south. Slowly but steadily, the south, which possessed most of the agriculture and most of the industry, became a client of the United States. For its part, the north became dependent on China and the Soviet Union as models of collectivism. Many in the West saw the coming struggle as one between ideologies. Others saw it as the perfect prelude to a Vietnamese civil war.

— ENDGAME —

Dien Bien Phu is a market town in an almost preposterously remote corner of northwest Vietnam. Common sources give its population as either nine thousand or twenty-two thousand (the former seems more likely to me). In 1953, however, it was so small it wasn't even considered a community and in fact didn't have a name. The phrase "Dien Bien Phu" translates roughly as "border-area administrative post." Few outsiders had ever heard of it. By the spring of 1954, however, it was a place very much in the news internationally.

France's eagerness to resume its lucrative control of Indochina at the end of the Second Wold War was stymied by the surprising, to French eyes, growth of the Viet Minh. As Ho Chi Minh was the political brain of the liberation movement, so Vo Nguyen Giap was the military one. Ted Morgan has written of Giap as "a man of action with a chess player's mind." Morgan, a senior American journalist and biographer, is himself, like Ho, a pseudonymous individual. Until he chose to become an American in the 1970s, he was Sanche de Gramont, a minor member of the lingering French nobility. (He selected "Ted Morgan" because it is an anagram of "de Gramont.") As a young man he was an intelligence officer in the French army, serving during the war in Algeria, where some of the soldiers he knew had survived the horrible fighting at Dien Bien Phu.

Few battles of the twentieth century were more resoundingly decisive or remain such powerful cautionary tales. What took place at Dien Bien Phu has become the subject of a vast literature in both celebratory Vietnamese and exculpatory French. In English, too, the topic keeps recurring in new books, both scholarly and popular. For years, the foremost work in English was Bernard Fall's *Hell in a Very Small Place: The Siege of Dien Bien Phu*. It was published in 1966, the year before its author was killed by a landmine while reporting the American War for the *New York Times*. More than four decades later came Morgan's *Valley of Death: The Tragedy at Dien Bien Phu That Led America into the Vietnam War*, a work whose subtitle says a great deal. I suppose that Morgan is still so French that his former nation's defeat seems a tragedy in more than just loss of life. But he may also have become so American that, like many others in the United States, he continues to seek precedents for what happened between 1965 and 1975. In any case, the two books are quite different. Fall loved military jargon and put far more effort into explaining logistics, for example, than ideology. In contrast, Morgan writes excellent journalistic prose and attempts the difficult of task of giving us the serious political context for the battle narrative.

What exactly went so wretchedly wrong for the French? Cultural condescension, certainly, but impatience, as well. The colonies were growing. In 1937, there were twenty thousand French people — the *colons* — in Vietnam and 19 million Vietnamese. By 1954 there were fifty thousand French and 25 million Vietnamese. The latter had stereotypes of the former: for instance, that of the big-bellied French officials and businessmen, growing rich and cruel on exorbitant taxation, rigidly imperial economics, and military might while living with their Vietnamese mistresses (*con gai*). For their part, the French saw the local population as backward and ignorant.

For a number of years the Viet Minh had been using standard guerrilla and terrorist tactics in both the cities and the rural areas, following methods learned by observing Mao Zedong. By 1953, however, the former ragtag guerrillas had become a formidable and highly disciplined army. We all know the platitude about the tendency of generals to refight the previous war. In this case, the previous war was the recently concluded one in Korea whose most glaring feature had come right at the beginning, in June 1950, when the North invaded the South by suddenly sending a "human wave" of 213,000 soldiers across the 38th parallel.

In Vietnam, the French, tired of the standard anti-colonial scrapping, and fearful that the Viet Minh would expand the war into neighbouring Laos, came up with a plan. They would fortify a strange misty valley a few miles from the Lao border. It was, and is, an elliptical plain made of red clay and surrounded on all sides by thick jungle and very high mountains. Such a tempting target was supposed to lure the Viet Minh into making a human-wave attack. The French imagined tens of thousands, maybe scores of thousands, of lightly armed *bo dois* charging over open ground, only to be mowed down by French artillery and air power in a single coup. The French believed they were well prepared for their mission. They had even brought along two field-brothels (*bordels militaires de campagne*) staffed with Algerian and Vietnamese women. But French G-2 work was very poor at best and almost non-existent at worst. They didn't know how many Vietnamese they were facing or where exactly these enemies were or even how they were armed. They knew only that the Viet Minh, who admittedly had no air force, likewise had no artillery to speak of, nor the skill to use it effectively if they had. These assumptions were mistaken. It was the French who became the sitting ducks.

The commander in Indochina was General Henri Navarre, who came from NATO headquarters in Europe. In his ignorance of Indochina, some saw the promise of a fresh perspective. He gave field command at Dien Bien Phu to an officer who had served under him in Italy during the Second World War: Colonel (but now, instantly, General) Christian Marie Ferdinand de la Croix de Castries, a cavalryman who had chosen to work his way up through the ranks rather than profit from the influence of his ancient military family. One of the officers Castries himself would most rely on at Dien Bien Phu was Colonel Charles Piroth. He, too, was a veteran of the Italian campaign, during which he had lost his left arm at the shoulder. He was an artilleryman whose task was to keep the Vietnamese human wave at bay until the optimal moment.

There were thirteen thousand French troops in all. Most of the rank-and-file were Algerians, Moroccans, or members of the Légion etrangère. Of this last group, many were ex-Nazis who considered questions about the previous decade somewhat impertinent. There were also some loyal tribal people, whom the French called autochthones. The French weren't fully aware that there were fifty thousand Vietnamese with as many again in reserve.

When the first French troops arrived by parachute in November 1953, during the dry season, they began building an airstrip and then, on either side of the Nam Yum River, nine defensive positions, what Morgan calls "this network of overlapping little fortresses, this labyrinth of barbed wire and sandbags...." The strongholds were given feminine fore-names, beginning with Anne-Marie and extending down the alphabet to Isabelle (and, contrary to legend, these were not the names of Castries's — or anybody else's — mistresses back in Paris). The defences were made of earth, concrete, and barbed wire, and were connected to one another by com-munication trenches. The building materials for these and for the all-important airstrip, not to mention all the weapons, ammunition, food, medical supplies — everything — had to be flown in, for although Hanoi was less than three hundred kilometres miles away, it was sixteen hours distant by road: a road controlled by the Viet Minh in any case. The airlift involved cargo planes acquired from the United States: C-47 Dakotas (in the early stages, they made eighty flights a day) and C-117 Flying Boxcars. This is when the trouble began.

The French foresaw no danger in occupying the lower ground rather than the higher, because they doubted that the Viet Minh had much artillery. The French possessed sixty guns. Although none of the Viet Minh pieces was as large as the heaviest French ones, they numbered two hundred in all, many of them from China. Similarly, the French couldn't accept that their enemy could move their big guns to the rugged mountaintops that surrounded the plain. But that's precisely what Giap did. He disassembled the field pieces as much as possible, cordelling them with ropes, dragging them centimetre by centimetre and metre by metre, using thousands of ungloved hands and sandaled feet; for, as Morgan has written, "although the French had tanks and airpower, it turned out that long lines of coolies were more dependable." The Viet Minh dug heavily disguised caves in which to conceal the cannon, bringing them out of hiding just long enough to do their work, before retracting them again. Also, they dug dummy caves at which they set off tiny explosions that mimicked muzzle flashes, tricking Colonel Piroth into wasting ammunition. They managed to render the French airfield useless and to prevent it from being repaired.

With terrible and inexorable efficiency, the guns in the mountains also destroyed the French expedition's fix-winged aircraft as well as helicopters and tanks. Food, ammunition, and medical supplies were running out as the casualties piled up, with no way to transport the wounded to Hanoi where they could be treated effectively. "By the end of March," Morgan wrote, "Dien Bien Phu was surrounded. The only way in was by parachute, and there was no way out." And as the cannon in the mountains pounded away, the Viet Minh down in the valley continually dug trenches of their own, moving ever closer. "Here, nine years into the nuclear age, was a return to siege warfare that went back to medieval times." Giap was a close student of the military classics — Napoleon, Clausewitz, and, most tellingly of all, the Marquis de Vauban, whose ideas had revolutionized siege three centuries earlier. For his part, Castries asked Hanoi to air-drop him four copies of the official manual of siege warfare published during the First World War.

The siege became a daily melodrama in the eyes of the world, including, of course, the United States, which, then as later, saw Ho Chi Minh not as a nationalist primarily, but as a tool of the Third International, bent on propagating global communism. When General Navarre took over in the region, insisting that the purpose of the campaign was to prevent the Viet Minh from attacking Luang Prabang, he told a subordinate, "We've had American generals, veterans of Korea, tell us how satisfied they were with our deployment. They invested a lot of money here and they didn't want us to lose."

His listener replied tactfully: "My only desire is to believe you, General." At one point Washington considered using nuclear weapons, but decided against the plan, fearing it would lead to sending U.S. ground forces into Vietnam.

A few French troops were getting in by parachute, but only a few. One sergeant wrote to his brother back home: "The Viets are two hundred metres from our barbed wire, hiding in trenches. They look at us. We look at them." He added: "On top of everything, we've run out of wine." A major with a safe desk job in Saigon learned that his wife had been lost at sea en route from France by steamship. In despair, he asked to be dropped into Dien Bien Phu. He was volunteering to commit suicide or, as he put it, "doing Camerone." The reference was to a famous nineteenth-century battle in Mexico in which an entire Légionnaire command was wiped out. Colonel Piroth no longer counted enough pieces of artillery to keep the enemy away or enough gunners left alive to man the guns if he still had them. He retreated to his bunker. Having only one arm, he found it difficult to load and cock his pistol, so he committed suicide by using his teeth to pull the pin on a grenade. Castries was, in Ted Morgan's words, "marinated in despondence." (Morgan enjoys culinary metaphors. A few pages on, a certain section of the battlefield is "truffled" with landmines.)

Most of French strongpoints were quite low, but there was one, code-named Dominique, that was a hundred or more metres high and of enormous circumference. Indeed, it is still the dominant geographical feature of Dien Bien Phu, over-looking the town. A full battalion was needed to defend it properly. Toward the end, it was manned by only two thin companies of Algerians, whom Castries considered unreliable in any case. "Better to obliterate a company than rout a battalion," Giap observed, as he tightened his stranglehold on each of the sorry outposts in turn. In Paris, the government began to look a bit wobbly. In Dien Bien Phu, the monsoon had begun. Mushrooms sprouted on the soldiers' boots after only twenty-four hours. The troops were out of almost everything. Both the living and the dead were sucked down into the mud.

On May 7, 1954, after fifty-six days of actual siege, General Castries surrendered. The most famous photograph of this French War is one of Viet Minh soldiers standing atop the round corrugated-iron roof of the general's bunker, waving their flag. Of the thousands of French troops who were taken prisoner, relatively few survived captivity and made it back to Europe or North Africa. Today, Dien Bien Phu's principal boulevard is named May Seventh Street.

The lessons of Dien Bien Phu are numerous and altogether obvious. At the end of his book, Morgan wrote:

> When he later read that some of Castries' men had died without showing any apparent wounds, Giap concluded that "their endurance had failed, because they did not know what they were fighting for." Navarre's defeat at Dien Bien Phu, Giap believed, had come from "an error in judgement in that he did not understand his adversary. He didn't realise it was a people's war." For the French elite troops, war was their profession. But what were they fighting for? Navarre's mistake was that he couldn't believe illiterate peasants could become good artillerymen, or that cadres who hadn't graduated from Saint-Cyr could solve strategic and tactical problems.

※

— TO HELL AND BACK —

Dien Bien Phu was made the capital of Lai Chau Province in 1993, but partly by default. The previous capital kept suffering devastating floods, caused mainly by deforestation, and may soon disappear altogether under the reservoir of a huge hydro dam. But of course, there was also another reason to elevate the status of DBP: patriotism. Giap's great victory is an event celebrated in school books, songs, and public art; in street names, memorials, and museums.

I met up with Christopher at the Hanoi airport on the specified day and off we went. What we saw almost immediately on landing is that the town's place in history has brought a certain amount of tourism, leading to such modest local institutions as the Lottery Hotel, the Construction Hotel, and the Beer Factory Guesthouse (none of which had room for us that day). Development has chewed up some of the edges of the battlefield, but not enough to keep visitors from getting a clear understanding of what the fighting must have been like. In contrast to China, which will often raze some historical site to build a modern replica of it, Vietnam tends to skilfully redo or replace lost or damaged elements without taking away from the original. Examples include some parts of the French blockhouses and bunkers. Others include the surprisingly deep trenches dug by both armies during their deadly and deadly serious game of cat-and-mouse.

In brief, DBP, though interesting, is a very small and isolated place with little commotion and less cosmopolitanism. Let me illustrate. I have one badly arthritic knee that will need replacing in the next few years. Until then, it acts up from time and time, buckling at inopportune moments. I had one such incident in DBP while climbing stairs at the only place with a vacancy: a combination hotel/massage parlour. The next day, I had to hobble about in search of ice with which to bring down the swelling. The only supply I found was in a mobile phone shop that also sold beer from an ancient fridge badly in need of defrosting. I paid the owner a few dong for the ice that had built up at the bottom. For days afterwards, I was a famous personage in town: the Westerner who spends good money on frozen water!

The community, whose local crops include rice and (in nearby tribal areas) opium, sits on red clay soil that reminded me of Prince Edward Island. In the dry season, the stuff is hard and dusty, but by the end of the rainy season has the consistency of pancake batter. For the past fifty-seven years, as it has dripped down the hillsides and embankments at the conclusion of each monsoon, it has revealed artifacts, including bits of human bone and sometimes teeth (French teeth, presumably). Without any effort whatever, we found three mud-caked brass cartridge casings. Two days before our arrival, a history buff from Britain discovered a French helmet. Inside was a scrap of scalp. But that was exceptional. After the French War, just as after the American War two decades later, the Vietnamese picked the countryside clean of valuable scrap metal.

The Englishman's discovery of the helmet was also somewhat out of the ordinary in that relatively few Western visitors spend time in DBP. Groups of Vietnamese school children on field trips — certainly. People with parents and grandparents buried in neat rows in the huge Viet Minh cemetery — of course. But the ranks of Frenchwomen widowed by Dien Bien Phu are pretty thin now, and the place is so far away and so difficult to reach even from the major Vietnamese cities. In fact, it's hard to get out of, as well.

I went with Christopher to meet some Black Thai women who lived nearby so he could see what common ground there might be between his contemporary Thai and their own dialect. The answer to the question, he said later, was that he could pick up some of what they were saying, but the extent of their mutual comprehension was probably the same as that between a modern Spaniard and some nineteenth- or even eighteenth-century Portuguese person. What I found interesting is that the women and young girls who were married wore their hair in a sort of giant beehive, through which they stuck a metal rod, somewhat like a giant knitting needle, to which a large coin was affixed. I could tell that the coins were replicas, made of cast aluminium. But one of the older wives (the youngest were only thirteen) had a genuine silver piece. I ask her permission to take a closer look. The lettering read INDOCHINE FRANÇAISE 50 PIASTRES and bore the date 1922. I imagine it had been handed down from grandmother to daughter to granddaughter.

Christopher had to be back in Bangkok on a certain morning so that he could say goodbye to his wife, Od, a human rights worker, before she left Thailand to participate in a conference. We had arranged a flight that would get us to Hanoi in time for him to make the Bangkok connection he needed. The tiny airport at Dien Bien Phu is built on the site of the French military airstrip whose destruction by Giap's artillery ensured the Viet Minh victory. After an hour or so on the ground, the empty Vietnam Airlines flight to Hanoi hadn't refuelled or allowed us few ticket-holders to board. Eventually, two workers came and removed everyone's luggage from the hold. Then mechanics, overseen by an official with a clipboard, began to disassemble part of the fuel system, leaving the components on the tarmac before quitting for the day. Eventually we heard an announcement that no other plane would be available for a day or two.

There being no bus and of course no train, Christopher and I decided to hire a taxi. The fare was astonishingly low, but the journey took the rest of the day and all night, over narrow mountain roads, unpaved for long stretches, with rock cliffs on one side and drops of maybe three hundred metres on the other — with no guard-rails or even white lines. The driver played loud Vietnamese rock on a CD player the whole time and honked the horn whenever he feared another vehicle was approaching in the darkness or when, as sometimes happens, a water buffalo, trying to stay cool, had taken refuge in a mud puddle in the middle of road. Veteran traveller that he is, Christopher crunched his hat into something resembling a pillow. "If we're still alive in the morning," he said, "then we'll know that we've made it." Whereupon he fell asleep.

We did indeed make it of course, but it was a wild night. We pulled up to the Hanoi airport with moments to spare as Christopher grabbed his rucksack and ran into the terminal, dishevelled-looking and with his shirttail hanging out. I still had a few more days to kill in Hanoi. I asked the driver if he could drop me off at the old Metropole Hotel, the equivalent of Bangkok's Oriental. He said yes, but got lost three or four times, for he was after all as much a stranger in Hanoi as I was, if not more so. In any case, I wasn't certain whether I'd be allowed in the dining room to treat myself to a fine breakfast. During the French Time, the Metropole was a great magnet for movie stars (Charlie Chaplin honeymooned there), Parisian debutantes, visiting mountebanks, French officials, and senior military officers, and I was rather scruffy in appearance by this time.

We passed along a street where there were several outdoor barbers plying their craft, and I got out there. I could see only the top half of the men's faces, as they wore the usual cotton masks because of the pollution. There was one obviously elderly fellow, frail-looking and with a head somewhat like a turtle's. I figured that he had probably gone through the French school system when he was a boy and that, between us,

we could have a halting conversation. In the end, though, neither of us seemed able to remember as much grammar as we
wished, and so I pulled out my Canadian passport and showed
him the photo. He nodded understandingly. I had taken the
seat looking somewhat like a holy picture of St. Jean Baptiste.
Now I left it looking like the expressionless dolt staring into
the lens at a little shop in a mall, having his passport photo
taken. I thanked the barber for his courtesy. He took off his
mask and smiled a nearly toothless smile. I thought he said,
"Le plaisir est le mien." The traffic was deafening.

George Fetherling has been a significant figure in the Canadian literary world for more than forty years. He has produced a long shelf of books as novelist, poet, memoirist, and writer of travel narratives. *Three Pagodas Pass*, *Running away to Sea*, and *One Russia, Two Chinas* are examples in the last category. He lives in Vancouver and Toronto.

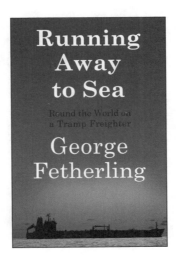

Running Away to Sea
Round the World on a Tramp Freighter
978-1550028539
$24.99

At a turning point in his life, George Fetherling embarked on an adventure to sail round the world on one of the last of the tramp freighters. The four-month voyage carried him thirty thousand nautical miles from Europe via the Panama Canal to the South Pacific and back by way of Singapore, Indonesia, the Indian Ocean, and Suez. Written with dash, colour, and droll humour, Fetherling's narrative is peopled by a rich cast of characters. The author captures the reality of life aboard a working cargo ship — the boredom, the seclusion, the differences of nationality and culture, but the routine of loneliness or tranquility is punctuated by moments of near-panic — shipboard fires, furniture-smashing storms, even a brush with pirates in the Straits of Malacca.

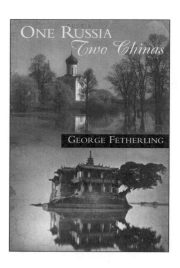

One Russia, Two Chinas
978-0888784339
$22.95

A travel narrative written over the course of ten years, *One Russia, Two Chinas* is about change and resistance to change in the postmodern world. In 1991, when the Soviet Union was about to morph into the Russian Federation, George Fetherling found himself in Moscow. He both marched with the workers in the last-ever Communist May Day parade and observed, at ground level, the new Russia's love of the marketplace. Fetherling then went overland to China. His entry point was Beijing, which at that moment was girding itself for the first anniversary of the Tiananmen Square massacre. Later that same year he journeyed to Taiwan, then in its final days as a dictatorship. This is old-fashioned travel writing, with vivid prose, bizarre characters, and crystallizing descriptions. But it's also a valuable document that freezes some important world events for close inspection.

Available at your favourite bookseller.

DUNDURN
www.dundurn.com

What did you think of this book?
Visit *www.dundurn.com* for reviews, videos, updates, and more!